idiot letters

Paul ... Street
CO 80907

Paul ... your letter
D... of letters. It
Share enthusias
Your suggestion of
might sugg
your boo
sup... manif
marketpl
the letter
...mage to the
...ould, however,
...terful stroke o
...to include in
...teurized, pro
...ashable
...se a...ard to
...ving the

The idea of ...s is s

...that I have re

29
USA

7.95
8.75
8.75

8.25
7.95
8.25
7.95
8.25
8.95
7.95
7.95
9.25
8.25
11.95
8.95

...coli
Sauce w/Peanuts
...ole
...Sauce in Brown Sauce
Flavor
...teed w/Fresh Tomato
Beef w/Black Bean Sauce
Beef w/Dry Bean Curd
Beef w/Fresh Chili Pepper
Chinese Broccoli
's Nest

idiot letters

One Man's Relentless Assault on **Corporate America**

P A U L   R O S A

A MAIN STREET BOOK
DOUBLEDAY
New York London Toronto Sydney Auckland

A MAIN STREET BOOK

PUBLISHED BY DOUBLEDAY

a division of Bantam Doubleday Dell Publishing Group, Inc.
1540 Broadway, New York, New York 10036

MAIN STREET BOOKS, DOUBLEDAY,
and the portrayal of a building with a tree
are trademarks of Doubleday, a division of
Bantam Doubleday Dell Publishing Group, Inc.

Library of Congress Cataloging-in-Publication Data
Rosa, Paul.
    Idiot letters: one man's relentless assault on
corporate America/Paul Rosa—1st ed.
        p.   cm.
    "A Main Street book."
    1. Letters—Humor. 2. Complaint letters—
Humor 3. Consumer complaints—Humor.   I. Title.
PN6131.R67 1995   94-38428
816′.54—dc20   CIP

ISBN 0-385-47508-X

Thanks to my sister, Nicki,
for believing in me.

To David Letterman,
for the inspiration.

To my agent, Lisa Bankoff,
for the expert guidance and good humor.

To the folks at Doubleday,
for the enthusiastic support...and the paycheck.

And to my cat, Jesse,
for teaching me the importance of good grooming.

...treet
Paul ... your letter
... CO 80907

... of letters. I
... share enthusia...
...our suggestion of
... might sugg...
... your boo...
... sup...mani...
...marketpl...
the letter...
...omage to the...
...ould, however, ...ly wr...
The idea of ...is s...
to include in ...
...asterful stroke o...
...eurized, pro...
...nshable i...
...se ...ward to
...iving the

that I have rich...

Pizza Hut®

9111 East Douglas
Wichita, Kansas 67201

*.. A Big Thank You for
a Preferred Customer!*

Mr. Paul Rosa
Or Current Resident
P.O. Box 9368
Colo. Springs, CO 80932

*This letter
started the
entire project!*

Dear Mr. Paul Rosa,

Maybe you can help me figure something out.

It's been a while since you ordered from a Pizza Hut® Restaurant or Delivery unit -- and that concerns me. You see, you're the kind of customer we'd like to see more often. So I asked myself some questions.

Now I know <u>you've tasted our pizza.</u> And if you're like the rest of America, you probably loved it. (We've been chosen America's favorite pizza place for 9 years running.)

Then I thought... maybe you're on a health kick. If so, you'll be happy to know that <u>we also deliver garden salad</u> with any pizza order.

And then it came to me... <u>you're looking for a bargain!</u> So I decided to send you these money-saving coupons. Use them for delivery or carry-out. Just call us at 719-634-1400.

Well... now that we've got that figured out, I look forward to hearing from you soon.

William McClave
William McClave
Division Vice President of Marketing

P.S. Be sure to try new BIGFOOT™ Pizza -- our enormous, rectangular shaped pizza perfect for big family and big party eating!

P.O. Box 9368
Colo. Springs, CO 80932
June 21, 1993

Mr. William McClave
Division Vice President of Marketing
Pizza Hut
9111 East Douglas
Wichita, KS 67201

Dear Mr. McClave,

I appreciate your concern regarding my recent failure to order a Pizza Hut Pizza, and was pleased to receive the (money-saving) coupons.

I was also complimented when you stated, "You're the kind of customer we'd like to see more often." What I would like to know, however, is which kind of customer *wouldn't* you like to see more often? I simply couldn't arrive at an answer, even after asking myself some questions (as you cleverly did).

Would you be so kind as to write to me and clear up this confusing matter? It's a puzzler!

Awaiting a sausage pizza as I type,

Paul Rosa

Paul C. Rosa

Pizza Hut, Inc., Western Division/15635 Alton Parkway/Suite 400/Irvine, CA 92718/Phone: (714) 727-9091
Fax: Operations (714) 727-9092, Mailroom/Finance (714) 727-9094, Development (714) 727-9096, Human Resources (714) 727-9095

July 15, 1993

Mr. Paul Rosa
P.O. Box 9368
Colo. Springs, CO 80932

Dear Mr. Rosa:

I thoroughly enjoyed your response to my letter to you and your follow-on question of "exactly which kind of customer <u>wouldn't</u> I like to see more often?"

I could, of course, give you an honest answer, but our corporate lawyers won't let me.

So instead, I'm signing off . . .

"Guilty As Charged",

William L. McClave
V.P. of Marketing - Western Division

WM/rlk

P.O. Box 9368
Colo. Springs, CO 80932
June 28, 1993

Maytag Customer Service
240 Edwards St., SE
Cleveland, TN 37311

Dear Customer Service Division,

For years I've watched your commercials on television featuring the Maytag repairman, who never has any work due to the dependability of the products he services. If this guy never has to do anything, why not *fire* his useless butt and pass the savings on to the consumers? We'd certainly appreciate it! Let me know what you think!

Wearing clean clothes,

Paul Rosa

Paul C. Rosa

MAYCOR ®

Appliance Parts & Service Co.

DIVISION OF
MAYTAG
CORPORATION

August 17, 1993

Mr. Paul C. Rosa
P.O. Box 9368
Colo. Springs, CO 80932

Dear Mr. Rosa:

I enjoyed our conversation last week regarding your suggestion that Maytag fire the lonely repairman.

It's a good cost savings idea. However, Maytag's customer service commitment requires that we keep at least one repairman trained and available ... just in case.

I hope that when you are in the market for appliances you will consider Maytag. Meanwhile, we thought that you might be able to use the enclosed Ol' Lonely sunshade (a small token of our appreciation for your interest in Maytag).

Thank you!

Sincerely,

Received a car SUNSHADE!

Dale Reeder
Director of Consumer Affairs

P.S. Please let us know if you are ever performing in the Chattanooga area ... we'll come to the show.

240 Edwards Street SE • Cleveland, TN 37311 • 615-472-3333 • FAX 615-478-0427
Providing Parts & Service for Maytag, Magic Chef, Jenn-Air, Admiral, Hardwick, Norge Appliances

P.O. Box 9368
Colo. Springs, CO 80932
July 2, 1993

The Mennen Co.
Morristown, NJ 07962-1928

Dear Mennen folks,

For years I've enjoyed your fine "Speed Stick" anti-perspirant and the way it keeps me feeling dry and smelling good (musk). Women have actually commented on my nice aroma, and my underarms have been virtually moisture free since I began using your product in high school thirteen years ago!

But recently I began to wonder where the perspiration **goes** that isn't "permitted" to exit naturally through my skin. Is it backing up dangerously somewhere inside my body, only to reach some sort of critical capacity when I'm fifty years old? And if I apply anti-perspirant before I play basketball, am I asking too much of my body not to sweat as it sees fit? Does the perspiration simply choose another exit (i.e. my feet)? That would be a relief!

So please get back to me about this. I've been worried that I may be doing great long-term harm to myself by using your product on a daily basis. Also, is it safe to use anti-perspirant on other body parts? I am cursed with a forehead that perspires heavily, and is at times embarrassing. Thanks for your swift response!

Feeling fresh but concerned,

Paul Rosa

Paul C. Rosa

The **MENNEN** *Company*

MORRISTOWN, NEW JERSEY 07962-1928
TELEPHONE 1-800-228-7408

December 9, 1993

Mr Paul Rosa
P.O. Box 9368
Colo. Springs, CO 80932

Dear Mr Rosa:

Thank you for contacting us with your question. We appreciate your interest in our company and its products.

Although we do not have the specific information you requested, enclosed is some material we think you will find interesting. We apologize for any inconvenience.

We appreciate your taking the time to contact us. Please accept the enclosed with our compliments.

Sincerely,

Claudio Pugliese
Consumer Representative
Consumer Affairs

CAP/nal

Enclosure
0079410B

P.O. Box 9368
Colo. Springs, CO 80932
July 3, 1993

Orkin Exterminating Co., Inc.
2170 Piedmont Rd., NE
Atlanta, GA 30324

Dear Orkin gang,

I would like to thank you for the excellent service you have extended to my family over the past few years. Whenever we've had roaches, fleas, ants, or rodents (rats!), the Orkin man (person) has descended on my home with a viciousness that is the terror of the pest world! The results can best be described as **"total annihilation!"**

But several things have puzzled me. First of all, why do the Orkin people (in person and in advertisements) always wear helmets? I don't see how it could possibly serve any purpose, unless the exterminator is clumsy and prone to banging his head on rafters, etc. Or perhaps it is meant to keep spiders and other miserable creatures from jumping in one's hair and (God forbid) <u>nesting</u>! That would be dreadful, don't you think? But both of these possibilities seem remote, indeed, and I remain perplexed! What's the answer?

Secondly, as a religious person (devout Lutheran) I have been concerned with the souls of the creatures slaughtered in my home. Do you think such animals can/do go to heaven, and if so, aren't we committing sinful acts? I suppose it's easy to dismiss it all by saying, "They're just miserable bugs and rodents! To hell with em'!" But isn't that an unfortunate stance? At what "point" does an animal's life merit concern? Pheasant? Emu? Pony? How do the Orkin people justify their jobs to themselves? Do some of you sleep fitfully or visit psychiatrists? How **do** you feel about these deaths?

Anyway, keep up the fine work but please get back to me about the two issues outlined above. Both have confused me for some time, and I'm sure your input would alleviate a great deal of concern!

No pests in *this* home,

Paul Rosa

Paul C. Rosa

P.S. Are rodents edible if well cooked?

PEST CONTROL
World's Best

July 8, 1993

Paul C. Rosa
P.O. Box 9368
Colo. Springs, CO 80932

Dear Mr. Rosa:

Thank you very much for your very kind letter about our service. We're certainly very proud to be able to serve you.

You raised two very interesting questions. I'll attempt to answer them.

1. "Why do the Orkin people (in person and in ads) always wear helmets?"

   Clumsy or not, it's very easy to get hurt by bumping one's head while inspecting and treating a home or business. We invest thousands of dollars in protective equipment for our employees in order to keep the risks of the job to an absolute minimum.

   We feel this is the right thing to do from a moral and a business perspective. We believe an aggressive safety program is just one of the subtle but powerful differences at Orkin.

   Thank you for noticing!!!

2. "Do you think such animals can/do go to heaven, and if so, aren't we committing sinful acts?"

   I think it's important that people realize Orkin professionals aren't out to blindly destroy any creature. Our work is very focussed and very directed. We target only those organisms that have become "out of place" and therefore in competition or conflict with the living space of our customers.

   We believe in the proper environment and situation, we don't have the right or need to affect any living creature. We don't get involved until circumstances necessitate intervention.

   We believe and practice our profession confident that our disciplined approach is warranted in the lives we have saved by our part in improving public health. Indeed there are numerous publications that support vector (pest) control as a requirement for reducing considerable pain and suffering.

Again, thanks for your kind words. And thanks especially for being our customer.

Joseph G. Harlow
Training Director

2170 Piedmont Road, N.E., Atlanta, Ga. 30324 (404) 888-2000
ANOTHER ROLLINS SERVICE

P.O. Box 9368
Colo. Springs, CO 80932
July 5, 1993

Consumer Affairs Dept.
Safeway Stores, Inc.
Oakland, CA 94560

Dear Safeway ,

Last night I enjoyed your "Bel-air Man Size Dinner" (Salisbury Steak), and found it delicious, indeed. The steak, gravy, mashed potatoes, corn in seasoned sauce, and chunky applesauce dessert were a pleasant surprise in today's age of bland TV dinners! Kudos on your fine accomplishment!

However, I noticed something which I found peculiar. On the box, in tiny letters, next to a large picture of the Salisbury Steak Dinner, appeared the words, **"Serving Suggestion."** Why is this here? Of course it is "suggested" that you eat the very food that comes in the box! Are there actually people who would cook your product, then grow confused and order a pizza?

Recently there has been an alarming increase in these "Serving Suggestion" appearances. I looked at my cereal box this week and saw a picture of a bowl of cereal with milk. Sure enough, in small print appeared the words, "Serving Suggestion." Haven't most people mastered the complicated world of breakfast cereals? Are we really in need of such instructions/suggestions?

Anyway, good people of Safeway, why *do* you put this on your product boxes? Is it for the benefit of the..."uneducated?" I just don't get it and would appreciate a swift reply. Your diligence in this matter is certainly appreciated!

Faithful to Safeway,

Paul Rosa

Paul C. Rosa

SAFEWAY INC.
2800 YGNACIO VALLEY ROAD
WALNUT CREEK, CA 94598

July 29, 1993

Mr. Paul Rosa
P.O. Box 9368
Colo. Springs, CO 80932

Dear Mr. Rosa:

We received your letter with your comments on the "Serving Suggstions" shown on our Bel-air Man Size Dinner packages.

The serving suggestions shown on cans and packages are meant to be helpful hints for the consumer much like that found in recipe books and other written food material.

Your comments have been forwarded to the Safeway personnel responsible for the product line as I am sure they will be interested in what you have to say.

Thank you for taking the time to write to us.

Very truly yours,

SAFEWAY INC.

Carolyn Bertson
Consumer Affairs

cc: R Calhoun
      J Templeton

P.O. Box 9368
Colo. Springs, CO 80932
July 6, 1993

Reckitt & Colman Household Products
A Division of Reckitt & Colman Inc.
Wayne, NJ 07474-0945

Dear Airwick Air Freshener rank and file,

Just a word to let you know how much I've appreciated your fine Airwick "Stick Ups" over the years! They've kept my house smelling fresh and clean for as long as I can remember. Recently I tried the "Country Potpourri" fragrance and was delighted with the results. Even my girlfriend (Cindy) commented on the delightful aroma. Your product truly does, as you claim, "Stop big odors in small places." Keep up the impressive work!

However, something has always struck me as a bit peculiar. On the back of the air freshener boxes appear the words, "Use Stick Ups in the following locations: Hampers, Cars, Under Sinks, Litter Boxes, Lockers, Garbage Pails, Near Toilets, Diaper Pails, and Closets." Each suggestion also features a picture of that location. Are there actually people who don't have the common sense to place an Air Freshener near something that smells bad? Might someone grow confused and place one next to an azalea in the living room, and then wonder why the bathroom **still** smells dreadful? Perhaps so. Maybe a person could buy a Stick Up because the cat's litter box stinks to high heaven, but when they return from the store they can't recall why they bought it. In this case, your suggestions would prove handy, indeed! Is this why you did it? Please let me know what's going on here, as it has confused me for some time. I look forward to hearing from you!

Fragrantly yours,

Paul Rosa

Paul C. Rosa

P.S. As someone who likes to bathe no more than twice a week, I was wondering if it would be safe to use a Stick Up on one's person (i.e. center of chest).

RECKITT & COLMAN

CONSUMER AFFAIRS   July 27, 1993

Mr. Paul C. Rosa
P.O. Box 9368
Colo. Springs, CO 80932

Dear Mr. Rosa,

We received your letter concerning Stick Ups, our concentrated air freshener. We're extremely pleased to hear you are satisfied with the effectiveness of this product.

In response to your comments regarding the pictures on the product packaging, we have found that in many instances visualization helps the consumer understand the uses of the product more clearly.

Comments from consumers are always welcome and we want you to know we appreciate the time you have taken to let us know your feelings. We value your patronage and hope you will use the enclosed coupons on future purchases of Stick Ups.

Your continued interest and support of our quality home care products are greatly appreciated. Thank you for taking the time to write.

                                        Sincerely,

                                        Ginger Newton

                                        Ginger Newton
                                        Consumer Affairs

/gn
enc.

P.O. Box 9368
Colo. Springs, CO 80932
July 8, 1993

Letters
Day One News Program
ABC News
30 W. 66th St.
New York, NY 10023

Dear ABC,

If a tree fell on Forrest Sawyer and no one was there to hear it, would he make a sound?

Anxiously awaiting your reply,

Paul Rosa

Paul C. Rosa

P.O. Box 9368
Colo. Springs, CO 80932
October 22, 1993

Forrest Sawyer
ABC News
30 W. 66th St.
New York, NY 10023

Dear Forrest,

Will you please finally answer my joke for you. It took me a long time to come up with it by myself.
Thanks. My father helped me with the computer though! Okay, here's the joke again:

If a tree fell on Forrest Sawyer and no one was there to hear it, would he make a sound?

Thanks for writing, Forrest, and please send a (XL) T-shirt for my dad if you can!

Sincerely,

Paul Rosa

Paul C. Rosa (4th Grade)

P.O. Box 9368
Colo. Springs, CO 80932
December 10, 1993

Forrest Sawyer
ABC News
30 W. 66th St.
New York, NY 10023

Dear Forrest,

It has now been five months since I first wrote to you with the joke I made up. The joke is:

If a tree fell on Forrest Sawyer and no one was there to hear it, would he make a sound?

As I mentioned in my second letter (October 22), it was not easy to think up a joke like this. My father thought it was really funny though, and he said I should send it to you to see what you think. I guess you hate my joke because you never wrote back to me in all this time! If you didn't like it you could have told me, but I'm mad that you couldn't at least answer me! Since I like to watch a lot of shows on ABC like "Day One," "Full House," "Home Improvement," and "Hangin' with Mr. Cooper," I think it would be great if ABC and you could be nicer to the viewers when they write letters!

I know you are very, very busy putting together interesting news segments, like when that train crashed down south, but is it so hard to write to someone within five months? Maybe you don't know what it's like to get your feelings hurt. I told some of the kids in my class (4th Grade, Mrs. Sterrinson) that you would write back and now they call me liar and stuff.

I'd really like to show Mark and Ray that I don't lie, so I'm sending you all the letters I've written, hoping that you will finally write to me, Mr. Sawyer! If you could just take a few minutes of time and say something about the joke, it would make me look good at school again! And I promise I won't bother you any more! Thanks a lot and keep up the good reports!

Sincerely,

Paul Rosa

Paul C. Rosa

P.S. I want to be a news man one day!

To Paul —
who comes up with
good riddles!

Forrest Sawyer

P.O. Box 9368
Colo. Springs, CO 80932
July 20, 1993

Marigold Soft Bathroom Tissue
Customer Service Dept.
Glencourt, Inc.
Walnut Creek, CA 94598-3592

Dear Restroom Folks,

It's been two years since I switched to your fine toilet tissue, and there has been no turning back! I find your product simple and inexpensive, but highly reliable. In this era of fancy, inefficient goods and services, your offering is a breath of fresh air, indeed. Have a drink on me (you've earned it!). It is with your expertise in mind that I also request some advice on the following topics:

How much toilet paper use is **too** much? I go through about twelve rolls a week, and it has occurred to me that I may be doing long-term harm to my...area. I average about ten "trips" to the bathroom a week, and thought I'd ask if you have any statistics on the subject of tissue use/overuse. Thanks for your help on this sensitive issue.

Secondly, is there a **better** way to unravel the roll from the spool. Some people unroll it so the paper unravels along the wall, while others prefer that it unravels closer to them. I find that it is harder for my cat (Jesse) to play with the roll if it hugs the wall. Which would you say is the most efficient? Have you conducted any surveys?

Finally, what is the deal with "scented" toilet paper? Sure, it's okay to smell good, but does anyone really benefit from smelling good...down yonder? I think not!

I have told my entire family (nine brothers and sisters) about your terrific product, and personally plan to use it until I die. I appreciate your time, and look forward to hearing from you concerning the issues I've discussed above.

Feelin' Fresh,

Paul Rosa

Paul C. Rosa

P.S. Are those cardboard tubes inside the tissue rolls recyclable? Can I send them to you?

 **SAFEWAY** INC.
2800 YGNACIO VALLEY ROAD
WALNUT CREEK, CA 94598

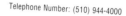

July 29, 1993

Mr. Paul Rosa
P.O. Box 9368
Colo. Springs, CO 80932

Dear Mr. Rosa:

We received your most recent letter with your kind words about our
Safeway Bathroom Tissue. We were pleased to have your comments as
we try very hard to provide our customers with the best possible
products under our Safeway private label product lines. It is
always nice to know that we have succeeded.

This product is part of our Safeway private label product line and
is made for us by an outside supplier. We do not have any
information on statistics on tissue usage. You might want to
contact one of the national brand suppliers of bathroom tissues to
determine whether they have done any such studies.

How you unravel the roll is strictly personal perference. There
is no one particular way that is better.

Scented paper is strictly a marketing situation. Apparently, it
has been found that many people like the scented paper. Maybe,
because the scent make the bathroom smell nice.

The tubes are recyclable because they are made of cardboard.

Thank you for taking the time to contact us and for taking an
interest in our product.

Very truly yours,

SAFEWAY INC.

Carolyn Bertson

Carolyn Bertson
Consumer Affairs

cc: R Calhoun
      J Templeton

P.O. Box 9368
Colo. Springs, CO 80932
August 15, 1993

Ms. Penny Sass
Consumer Relations Manager
Scott Paper Company
Scott Plaza
Philadelphia, PA 19113

Dear Ms. Sass (or "Penny," if that's all right),

Hello, Philadelphia! I grew up in Pennsylvania (Pittsburgh) and still have some very warm memories of the Keystone State. In the winter, my family would often go to Seven Springs Ski Resort and have a terrific time! After graduating from Penn State, I was somewhat saddened to accept a position in Colorado (I work for a company that manufactures manhole covers and quality mufflers).

But, for heaven's sake, Penny, I digress! I recently contacted Safeway, Inc., who distributes Marigold Bathroom Tissue. I posed several questions and was promptly and efficiently answered. One of my questions remains unanswered though, and it was suggested by Safeway (Carolyn Bertson in Consumer Affairs) that I "contact one of the national brand suppliers of bathroom tissue." That's why I am writing to Scott Paper Company! I have enclosed a copy of Carolyn's letter to confirm my story.

As I mentioned to Safeway, I use about twelve rolls of toilet paper a week, and it has occurred to me that I may be "overdoing" it. As I make about ten "trips" to the bathroom a week, this averages out to 1.2 rolls per trip. I asked them (and now I ask you) if there have been any studies done on the subject of tissue use/overuse. It worries me that I may be doing long-term harm to myself. If such a study exists, would you be so kind as to send it?

And while I have your attention, here are a few more questions that "came" to me recently:

1. Have you considered creating a toilet paper with pictures of unpopular
   historical figures (i.e. Hitler, Genghis Khan, Lucifer) printed on it?
2. What's the deal with those European bidets?
3. When was toilet paper invented (and by whom), and what was used
   before this historical breakthrough? Leaves? Wool? Nothing (yuck!)?

I know I've asked some unusual questions, but my heart is in the right place. If you could find the time to write to me, I'd be grateful! By the way, Penny, do you have any siblings named Nickel, Dime, or Quarter (I'm working on a stand-up comedy routine)?

Flushed with excitement,

Paul Rosa

Paul C. Rosa

SCOTT

October 13, 1993

Mr. Paul C. Rosa
P.O. Box 9368
Colo. Springs, CO 80932

Dear Mr. Rosa:

Thank you for your inquiry regarding bathroom tissue.

As for usage, we checked with our Marketing Research department and learned that our data indicates that an average buyer purchases 94 rolls a year. This is based on an average household with 2.2 kids and normal usage.

We do not anticipate any problem with your using any of our brands at the rate that you do. The dyes and chemicals used in our products have been tested and approved for our use. They undergo a very strict internal chemical control and approval process to protect the employee, the customer, the environment and assure compliance with legal requirements. Our only concern would be one of economics for you since you are having to purchase so many rolls per week.

Regarding historical figures, we do add new colors and designs to our product line from time to time. These changes are based, primarily, on consumer preferences which we obtain from market research studies. We cannot assure you that we will ever offer this feature.

Enclosed is a copy of our pamphlet, "The History of Bathroom Tissue" which we hope you will enjoy reading.

We appreciate this opportunity to communicate with you.

Sincerely,

Maxine C. Johnson
Senior Consumer
Relations Representative

/eh

Enclosure

P.O. Box 9368
Colo. Springs, CO 80932
July 22, 1993

The Quaker Oats Company
Customer Service
P.O. Box 049003
Chicago, IL 60604-9003

Dear Morning Friends,

For years I've enjoyed your fine breakfast products and the subsequent health benefits!
You offer the American people not only a delicious start to their days, but a tasty one as
well! And that's not easy to do in today's drive-thru world. You each deserve a hug!

Furthermore, I've always enjoyed your commercials featuring the versatile Wilford
Brimley. He's an excellent spokesman and a fine actor! Did you see him in this
summer's blockbuster film, "The Firm?" An Oscar perhaps? I'd say so!

But then it hit me: Does Mr. Brimley *really* eat oat meal? He seems a little...portly, and
the possibility of a different breakfast agenda seems at least conceivable! If he preaches
the virtues of a healthy breakfast, but then devours a four-egg cheese omelet with Spam,
isn't that hypocritical? Do you supervise his breakfast intake to insure the integrity of
your commercials? Is Mr. Brimley's weight monitored from time to time? Have you
included a "Thigh Master" among his contract perks? It seems like a sound investment
for all concerned!

Anyway, please let me know about this situation. I thoroughly enjoy your cereals, but
simply can not support a company that stretches the truth. A comforting letter would
make a world of difference and return me to my relaxed breakfast moods. Thank you!

Happily Munching,

Paul Rosa

Paul C. Rosa

P.S. Please ask Mr. Brimley to drop me a line...if he has the time!

The Quaker Oats Company
P.O. Box 9003
Chicago, Illinois 60604-9003

August 4, 1993

Mr. Paul Rosa
P.O. Box 9368
Colo. Springs, CO 80932

Dear Mr. Rosa:

Thank you for contacting us.

Whenever a consumer takes the time to contact us, we are eager to respond. Please be assured that your point of view has been shared with the appropriate corporate management. It will be given careful consideration and kept in mind for the future.

The comments of our consumers are always welcome and we appreciate having them on record.

Annmarie Marongiu
Consumer Response Specialist
Consumer Response Group

AM/LCM

QUAKER

We're happy to
send the information
we currently
have available.

CONSUMER AFFAIRS CENTER
THE QUAKER OATS COMPANY

P.O. Box 9368
Colo. Springs, CO 80932
August 9, 1993

Annmarie Marongiu
Consumer Response Specialist
Consumer Response Group
The Quaker Oats Company
P.O. Box 9003
Chicago, IL 60604-9003

Dear Annmarie,

Thanks for your speedy response to my letter of July 22! It is Quaker Oats' devotion to the consumer that has made them *the* cereal company of the 90's (and beyond!).

However, I have cause for anger. Maybe your response was so swift because none of my questions were even addressed! It seems like I just got one of those "form letters" that makes a man feel vacant and lonely inside. Doesn't a sincere letter deserve a similar reply? Or has the era of concern vanished with my Grandpa Tim (1908-1991)?

Although I am a busy man - I farm 45 acres of turnips - I've decided to re-submit my letter, and urge you to address (at least) my *major* questions:

- Does Mr. Brimley really eat oat meal?
- Is his weight monitored to insure the integrity of the commercials?

I appreciate your diligence in this matter, Annmarie, and look forward to another swift response (written, as I own no phone).

Cereal is good,

Paul Rosa

Paul C. Rosa

P.S. My nephew (Ray, age 9) told me this joke:

Q. What do you call someone who throws away a new box of Quaker Oats?
A. A "Cereal Killer!"

Cute, huh? Do you know any jokes?

P.O. Box 9368
Colo. Springs, CO 80932
September 27, 1993

Annmarie Marongiu
Consumer Response Specialist
Consumer Response Group
The Quaker Oats Company
P.O. Box 9003
Chicago, IL 60604-9003

Dear Ms. Marongiu (Is that Swedish?),

The Quaker Oats Company (and you) have treated me disrespectfully, and a cereal switch appears imminent. If my question is not answered by Halloween, I will sadly begin purchasing Cheerios, Grape-Nuts, or Raisin Bran. My nephew (Ray), who offered the "cereal killer" joke (see letter 2), asked me, "Why doesn't Quaker Oats listen to you, Uncle Paul?" Do you know what I say, Ms. Marongiu? I say, "I don't know, Ray. Maybe they're busy." He can tell I'm lying and it breaks my heart, damn it!

For the last time, I ask you, "Does Mr. Brimley *really* eat oat meal?"

Please check a box:

☐ yes
☐ no

I have enclosed a self-addressed stamped envelope to make it even simpler to answer me. My first two letters are also included for your perusal. I've contacted the Better Business Bureau, telling them how impossible it has been to get some results. They are waiting to hear further details.

I'm not often so aggressive, Ms. Marongiu, but this is an exception! As an Air Force Veteran, I demand respect! Please return this letter immediately (with a box checked!), and allow me to again embrace Quaker Oats! Cheerios are barely edible!

Hoping for peace,

Paul Rosa

Paul C. Rosa

P.S. A (XL) T-shirt would be a terrific gesture of good will!

P.O. Box 9368
Colo. Springs, CO 80932
October 3, 1993

Mr. Wilford Brimley
C/O Screen Actors Guild (SAG)
5757 Wilshire Blvd.
Los Angeles, CA 90036

Dear Mr. Brimley,

First of all, I wish to thank you for the *years* of memorable roles you've effectively tackled in films ("The Firm," "Absence of Malice," "Cocoon," and more). I think you have a good shot at an Oscar for your work in "The Firm!" My fingers are crossed for you, my friend.

As the enclosed letters detail, I have been in contact with The Quaker Oats Company for three months , unsuccessfully trying to get an answer to one simple question:

"Does Wilford Brimley *really* eat oat meal?"

In my first letter (July 22, 1993), I said that you seemed a little portly (no offense intended) and might be eating "other things." I also asked if your weight was monitored to insure the integrity of the commercials. Soon I received a form letter from the Consumer Response Group (Annmarie Marongiu), assuring me that my "point of view has been shared with the appropriate corporate management." What point of view, damn it? I asked a *question*!

Since then I've written two more letters (August 9 and September 27, 1993) trying to have my simple query answered. In the last letter, I only asked them to check a box (yes or no), to indicate whether you eat oat meal. But still they ignore me! Like your character in "Absence of Malice," I fervently want the truth so I can get on with my life! For this reason, I have decided to contact you directly and ask, once and for all, "Do you eat oat meal, sir?" I know you will be far more conscientious and I expect a reply shortly. A self-addressed, stamped envelope (SASE) is enclosed for your convenience. By the way, my wife saw you in the Colorado Springs Airport last year, and said you looked "handsome!"

A movie fan,

Paul Rosa

Paul C. Rosa

P.S. Do you sell (XL) T-shirts?

No Reply

P.O. Box 9368
Colo. Springs, CO 80932
September 27, 1993

Annmarie Marongiu
Consumer Response Specialist
Consumer Response Group
The Quaker Oats Company
P.O. Box 9003
Chicago, IL 60604-9003

Dear Ms. Marongiu (Is that Swedish?),

The Quaker Oats Company (and you) have treated me disrespectfully, and a cereal switch appears imminent. If my question is not answered by Halloween, I will sadly begin purchasing Cheerios, Grape-Nuts, or Raisin Bran. My nephew (Ray), who offered the "cereal killer" joke (see letter 2), asked me, "Why doesn't Quaker Oats listen to you, Uncle Paul?" Do you know what I say, Ms. Marongiu? I say, "I don't know, Ray. Maybe they're busy." He can tell I'm lying and it breaks my heart, damn it!

For the last time, I ask you, "Does Mr. Brimley *really* eat oat meal?"

Please check a box:

☒ yes
☐ no

I have enclosed a self-addressed stamped envelope to make it even simpler to answer me. My first two letters are also included for your perusal. I've contacted the Better Business Bureau, telling them how impossible it has been to get some results. They are waiting to hear further details.

I'm not often so aggressive, Ms. Marongiu, but this is an exception! As an Air Force Veteran, I demand respect! Please return this letter immediately (with a box checked!), and allow me to again embrace Quaker Oats! Cheerios are barely edible!

Hoping for peace,

Paul Rosa

Paul C. Rosa

P.S. A (XL) T-shirt would be a terrific gesture of good will!

P.O. Box 9368
Colo. Springs, CO 80932
July 24, 1993

Victoria's Secret
Customer Service
P.O. Box 16589
Columbus, OH 43216-6589

Dear Lingerie Leaders,

My girlfriend has been receiving your catalog for six years, and we *both* thoroughly enjoy the photographs. Barbara (my girlfriend) regularly orders an item or two, and it truly spices up our "private" life! When she recently bought the Genevieve bra and bikini, I almost lost my mind! Wow, this is living!

I think the models in the catalog are, for the most part, lovely, but not diverse enough. For instance, why aren't there any *heavy* models? My girlfriend weighs about 220 pounds and she is the sexiest woman I know! She gives a whole new meaning to "stretch fabric!" And why aren't there any really *short* models? I once dated a girl who stood 4'7", and she was a voluptuous angel. Finally, I never see any women in your catalog with extremely big feet or noses. Believe it or not, these are tremendous turn-ons for a lot of fellas!

There are many types of women in this world, and it seems a shame to concentrate on only one shape. I think you'll find that a wider variety of models will increase your sales by as much as 20%! So what do you think of my idea? Could you try to include some of the "types" I mentioned above in future catalogs? I'd be thrilled. And so would my girlfriend! I look forward to your speedy reply!

Tryin' to help,

Paul Rosa

Paul C. Rosa

P.S. Who is Victoria, and what is her secret?

P.O. Box 9368
Colo. Springs, CO 80932
September 13, 1993

Victoria's Secret
Customer Service
P.O. Box 16589
Columbus, OH 43216-6589

Hello, Garter Gang!

It has been seven weeks since I wrote to you, and I'm beginning to think a reply isn't coming! Since my girlfriend (Barbara) spends several hundred dollars a year on your superb products, I assumed a response wasn't too much to hope for. Perhaps I was wrong. With Barbara at my side -she's wearing a Victoria's Secret bra- I am now re-submitting my letter.

If it is too much trouble to read the letter, I can summarize it with two questions: Why aren't there any women in your catalogs who are extremely short or heavy? Why don't any of the women in your catalogs have large feet or noses? There, that's not too tough, is it?

Since I sent my last letter, however, I've come up with a few more questions:

- Have you considered offering garter belts specifically for *men*?
- Do most of the Victoria's Secret models floss?
- Is Sally Struthers a customer (I have a big crush)?

I hope this time I'll be treated with a little more respect. Please write to me soon and address my above queries! By the way, Barbara is "gearing up" for her huge autumn lingerie order from your company; I can't wait!!!

Love is in the air,

Paul Rosa

Paul C. Rosa

P.S. Please send a (XL) T-shirt.

P.O. Box 9368
Colo. Springs, CO 80932
October 17, 1993

Victoria's Secret
Customer Service
P.O. Box 16589
Columbus, OH 43216-6589

Dear negligent customer service department,

I am a proud American. I work extremely hard at my job as a livestock control analyst, I obey the law, and I promptly pay my taxes. I am also a devoted (divorced) father who has little spare time for frivolous activities. But I am so upset with you folks that I felt the need to contact you for the *third time in three months*!

I wrote for the *first* time on July 24, 1993, asking various questions about the lingerie models you use in your catalogs. I asked why you never used ladies who are larger, shorter, etc., and mentioned that such untraditional figures are a big turn-on for fellows like me. My girlfriend's devotion to your products was also discussed.

Seven weeks passed with no reply, so I wrote again (September 13, 1993), politely asking for a response to my queries. I also took the opportunity to ask several more (admittedly obscure) questions. Then I patiently waited for a response.

It is now five weeks later (*twelve weeks overall!*), and you *still* haven't found it necessary to write! What sort of an organization is it that ignores its customers' inquiries completely? I simply don't understand and feel somewhat depressed, but I've decided to (perhaps foolishly) write one more time. I am re-submitting the aforementioned letters for your review and urge you to *finally* give me some attention. As a young man, growing up in Bainbridge, GA (pop. 10,553), I was taught the meaning of respect and request that others treat me the same way I treat them! And while battling chronic bouts of migraine headaches (1984-1987) I learned the importance of patience and faith (I'm an Anglican).

So let's put this tedium behind us once and for all, folks. Kindly review the enclosed letters and promptly respond to them. I recognize that some of my questions are a bit...odd, so answer only those you are comfortable with. I am enclosing a self-addressed, stamped envelope (SASE) for your convenience. Good day and God bless.

Somewhat hurt,

Paul Rosa

Paul C. Rosa

VICTORIA'S SECRET
C A T A L O G U E

October 29, 1993

Paul Rosa
P.O. Box 9368
Colo. Springs, CO 80932

Dear Mr. Rosa:

I am in receipt of your recent letter and copies of your previous ones and I apologize for our failure to respond to you within a reasonable time.

Thank you for your suggestions regarding our models. We are always interested in the opinions and concerns of our customers.

Victoria's Secret employs models whose actual size is appropriate for our merchandise. We offer garments in the size 2-14 range and the models are wearing the actual merchandise available through our book. Lane Bryant, a former division of The Limited, publishes a catalogue and utilizes models of appropriate proportions to showcase their merchandise, which is offered in a larger size range. If you would like to be placed on their mailing list, you may call 1-800-477-7070 and a representative will be happy to accommodate you.

We currently offer a limited selection of men's wear, including boxers, briefs, pyjamas and robes. We do not have plans presently to expand that line to include additional merchandise for men.

I regret that I am unable to answer your questions regarding our particular models or customers. Out of respect for their privacy, we do not divulge that type of information.

I hope this information is helpful to you, Mr. Rosa. We value you as a customer and look forward to continuing to serve you.

Sincerely,

Denise Kerkovich

Denise Kerkovich
Senior Customer Service Specialist

P.O. Box 9368
Colo. Springs, CO 80932
July 25, 1993

The Upjohn Company
Dermatology Division (Rogaine with Minoxidil)
Customer Service
Kalamazoo, MI 49001

Dear Scalp Savers,

I am still on Cloud 9 because my once bald dome is now sporting a glorious, fuzzy growth! When I was twenty-two I began to lose my hair, and never dreamed it would one day, like a lost love, return! But after six months of diligently applying Rogaine to my shining head, I was rewarded with the aforementioned result. At age forty-one I am reborn! Even my wife seems to have a fresh spring in her step since the change. You folks are saviors!

It is with your obvious competence in mind that I write further, concerning a different (but similar) subject. As I age, while hair departs one part of my body (skull), it seems to tragically reappear on others (ears, nose, shoulders, and buttocks). I remove the offending follicles with frequent plucking and shaving, but they seem to return faster than I can attack them! Are your scientists working on any ointments that would "*block*" these evil growths in areas where they are unwelcome, and have them magically resurface on one's head? Perhaps that could be your next big project. I bet millions of men (and a few women) would applaud such a breakthrough. I sure would, as I'm tired of being the "gorilla at the beach!" Let me know the Upjohn agenda, please.

Finally (and this is most embarrassing), is it safe to use a bit of Rogaine in the...pubic area? I don't have the "thatch" I did as a lad, and would like to get it back. Is there much thinning of pubic hair in the general public? I guess it really isn't a big deal, but it's important to me!

Please let me know about the above queries as soon as possible, and I will continue to smear your product into my (improving) head! God bless you people!

Love,

Paul Rosa

Paul C. Rosa

P.S. Do you have any Rogaine T-shirts (XL)? I would love to contribute to the success of a product as fine as yours!

P.O. Box 9368
Colo. Springs, CO 80932
August 16, 1993

E. A. (what's that *short* for?) Miller
Executive Director, U.S. Marketing
The Upjohn Dermatology Division
P.O. Box 9030
Opa Locka, FL 33054-9944

Dear E. A. (Ethan Allen?),

I was impressed that you responded to my letter of July 25 in only three weeks. It is Upjohn's concern for the public that makes them the leaders in the war against hair loss and its accompanying despair!

But I was angry, nay livid, that my passionate letter warranted only a "form letter" in return, leaving my detailed questions and concerns *completely* unanswered! As I have spent hundreds of dollars on Rogaine Topical Solution, I assumed that my (time consuming) letter would at least be read! Apparently I was wrong, and I'm considering abandoning your product as you've abandoned me. A head of hair isn't worth losing my self-respect over, damn it!

I was sure my letter went unread because I received a list of local doctors, a $10 introductory coupon, and an informative brochure. I stated earlier that I have used Rogaine for some time, so why would I have any need for this "first-timer" stuff?! As I am impressed (for the most part) with Upjohn, I've decided to re-submit my first letter and briefly outline its points below:

- Are your scientists working on any ointments that would "*block*" hair in areas where they are unwelcome (buttocks, nose, etc.), and have them magically resurface on one's head?
- Is it safe to use Rogaine in the pubic area?
- Do you have any Rogaine T-shirts (XL)?

Now that I have outlined my previous letter (and re-submitted it!), I would hope that I could finally get a *proper* response! I am the **President** of the Colorado Bald Man Association (C.B.M.A., membership 2,256), and that's a lot of Rogaine being used, if you get my drift! As I am recovering from throat surgery, and speak with great difficulty, I would appreciate a *written* response. Thank you.

Pensively,

Paul Rosa

Paul C. Rosa, C.B.M.A. President

THE UPJOHN COMPANY

7000 PORTAGE ROAD
KALAMAZOO, MICHIGAN 49001-0199, U.S.A.

THE UPJOHN DERMATOLOGY DIVISION
KAREN L. LASSEN
Customer Service Administrator
TELEPHONE: *(616) 329-5743*
FACSIMILE: *(616) 329-8779*

August 31, 1993

Mr. Paul C. Rosa
P.O. Box 9368
Colo. Springs, CO 80932

Dear Mr. Rosa:

Your letter to E.A. (Ellen A.) Miller, The Upjohn Company, was forwarded to me for response.

First, please allow me to apologize for the confusion when you received another information packet for ROGAINE® instead of a response to your letter. When your letter arrived at our fulfillment house, they forwarded it to me, and by mistake, entered you into the computer to receive another information packet.

The response to your letter was delayed because I was waiting to talk to our Director of New Product Planning about permanent hair removal research. However, he has been out of the office for the past two weeks. According to the Director of New Product Planning, Upjohn did conduct some pilot studies to look at potential treatments for excessive hair growth. Unfortunately, those compounds did not work. Therefore, the company is not studying permanent hair removal treatments at this time. However, our researchers are continuing to look for other compounds that might be possible treatments for excessive hair growth.

With regards to using ROGAINE in the pubic region, we don't know if ROGAINE would be safe or effective if used in this area of the body. Our studies with ROGAINE were conducted on the crown of the scalp only. Therefore, we cannot recommend that ROGAINE be used on other parts of the body.

Last, you asked if we had ROGAINE t-shirts available; unfortunately, we don't. We had t-shirts when Upjohn sponsored the Chicago Marathon and the Los Angeles Marathon. Last year was the last time we sponsored those races, therefore, we didn't order extra t-shirts as we have in the past. However, enclosed you will find a compact road atlas. We hope this useful.

Mr. Rosa, again, we apologize for the confusion regarding the response to your letter, but thank you for taking the time to write us and for your interest in ROGAINE.

Sincerely,

Karen L. Lassen

enc.

P.O. Box 9368
Colo. Springs, CO 80932
August 1, 1993

Customer Service
WM. Wrigley Jr. Co.
Chicago, IL 60611

Dear Chewing Family,

Since the 1960's, I've faithfully chewed your fine gum products, and I must say it's made my life a whole lot better! I've chewed over 29,000 sticks of gum in this period, and was wondering if this is a record pace (I'm only 31 years old!)? I'd be thrilled if it was!

Recently I tried Wrigley's "Big Red," and have decided to chew it *exclusively*! Its smooth taste and pleasurable texture have won me over. I'm so impressed with it, that my average daily consumption (A.D.C.) has soared from 3.2 to 3.6 sticks a day (figures rounded off). Impressive, huh? Given that I live to be 75 years old - which is about average - my total gum consumption could top 86,000 sticks! Do you keep any statistics on gum intake?

Anyway, today, as I was enjoying my fourth Big Red stick of the day, I accidentally swallowed it! In 25 years of chewing this has *never* happened to me, so needless to say I am frantic, indeed! What will become of the gum? I asked my sister (Nicki) what would happen, and she said I would need surgery or my intestines would be heavily damaged. I don't know if she's telling the truth, but it doesn't hurt to ask. Am I in danger?!

Also, I've enjoyed your magazine ads which encourage: "When you can't smoke, enjoy pure chewing satisfaction." Does this work the *other* way too? If I'm caught somewhere without my beloved gum (unlikely), do cigarettes taste about the same? I've never smoked, but I'm willing to give it a try if it's comparable. What do you say?

So, that's all for now. Please get back to me quickly about these issues, especially the gum swallowing scare! In the meantime, I'll keep on chewin'!

Jaws of iron,

Paul Rosa

Paul C. Rosa

P.S. Is gum chewing encouraged at Wrigley Field?

Wm. WRIGLEY Jr. Company

WRIGLEY BUILDING • 410 N. MICHIGAN AVENUE
CHICAGO, ILLINOIS 60611

Telephone: 644-2121
Area Code 312

WHOLESOME · DELICIOUS · SATISFYING

August 10, 1993

Mr. Paul C. Rosa
P.O. Box 9368
Colo. Springs, CO 80932

Dear Paul:

Thank you for writing to let us know how much you enjoy Big Red
gum and to let us know you are concerned about the digestibility
of chewing gum. We appreciate your taking time to write.

Many people seem to harbor misconceptions about chewing gum, and
we've received many letters over the years asking about the
digestibility of our product. To give you some background,
chewing gum is made of five basic ingredients -- sugar, corn
syrup, softeners, flavors and gum base (the insoluble part that
puts the "chew" in chewing gum). The first four ingredients are
soluble and are extracted from the gum as you chew. Gum base is
not, and if it is swallowed, it simply passes through one's
system as other roughage does. This normally takes only a few
days.

Incidentally, chewing gum is a food product, so all ingredients
used in it may be used in chewing gum in compliance with U.S.
Food and Drug Administration regulations. In other words,
nothing in chewing gum may be considered harmful.

I'm enclosing a copy of <u>The Story of Chewing Gum and the Wm.</u>
<u>Wrigley Jr. Company</u>, which I hope you'll enjoy reading. We hope
you will continue to enjoy Wrigley brands. Thanks again for
writing.

Sincerely yours,

WM. WRIGLEY JR. COMPANY

Barbara C. Zibell
Consumer Affairs Administrator

BCZ/sl
Enclosure

P.O. Box 9368
Colo. Springs, CO 80932
August 3, 1993

Customer Service
Procter & Gamble
Ivory Soap
Cincinnati, OH 45202

Dear Lather Legions,

Since I was a small child, I have showered and bathed with your terrific soap. I estimate that I have used it over 10,000 times, and love the way it makes my skin feel. I think it's fair to say that Ivory Soap is as American as Ben Franklin or his kids (if he had any)! I had planned to be faithful to your product until I died, but all that has changed.

Last week, as I was carefully inspecting an Ivory wrapper, I read, "99 & 44/100% pure." I instantly wandered what the remaining 56/100% consisted of. When I asked my brother (Bill), he said that he heard that the remaining portion consisted of elephant tusks and rhinoceros horns (hence, the name **IVORY!**). I was aghast! I have already stopped using your soap -**COAST** is pretty good- until I learn the facts! Enough animals have been slaughtered!! So, what gives? What *is* the mysterious (impure) ingredient that you refuse to divulge?

Please get back to me at once, as I am pretty upset about my possible lifetime support of animal abuse. When I learn otherwise, I would be proud to return to Ivory for life!

Anxious suds,

Paul Rosa

Paul C. Rosa

P.S. I switched from Ivory to Coast, as it seemed like a clever move (Ivory Coast, get it?)

Procter&Gamble

The Procter & Gamble Company
Public Affairs Division
P.O. Box 599, Cincinnati, Ohio 45201-0599

September 2, 1993

MR PAUL ROSA
P.O. Box 9368
Colo. Springs, CO 80932

DEAR MR ROSA:

Thank you for asking about the ingredients in Ivory soap. This product does not contain elephant tusks or rhinoceros horns. You can be assured Procter & Gamble is careful in reviewing the ingredients we use in our products. I'm enclosing written information about the ingredients in Ivory soap. I hope you will continue to be a loyal Ivory consumer in the future.

I hope this information is helpful. Thanks again for writing.

Sincerely,

Lisa Simpson

Lisa Simpson
Consumer Services

P.O. Box 9368
Colo. Springs, CO 80932
August 3, 1993

Consumer Information
Oil-Dri Corporation of America
Cat's Pride Premium Cat Litter
520 North Michigan Ave.
Chicago, IL 60611

Dear Cat Lovers,

For the first ten years of my cat's life, it was a living *hell* trying to get her to use her litter box! Whenever she would get the call from nature (night or day), she would howl until someone would let her out. Needless to say, this made my wife (Vicki) and I extremely angry, as we were often woken from a sound slumber, or interrupted during...Matlock. We tried many litter boxes (circular, octagonal, etc.) and brands of cat litter, but she simply refused to cooperate. We were actually tempted to give her away, but simply love her too much - she was a gift from my mother (Irene).

This all changed a few months ago when, at wits' end, we tried Cat's Pride on the suggestion of a friend (Max). Well, we were delighted, nay *ecstatic,* when Jesse -without hesitation- stepped into the litter box and "unloaded." After ten years of treating her box like it was filled with glass chips, she finally found something she likes! And her attitude hasn't changed! Since that day she has ventured to the basement on a daily basis to fulfill her duty. The increased cleaning chores on our part are quite acceptable, considering the time now saved from letting her in and out and in and out and.... I don't know what's in that stuff, but it has done the impossible: changed the lifestyle of a ten year old cat (70 to you and me)! Yippee!

The only thing I thought was a bit odd was the name **"CAT'S PRIDE**." I can understand that your *corporation* would be proud of this cat litter, but a cat? When Jesse is heaving and straining in her box, I don't think *pride* is one of her sentiments. In fact I don't think cats are proud of anything at all, ever! So, why did you choose this name? It seems wrong to suggest what cats are "feeling" without offering any proof. Isn't that dishonest?

In conclusion, I am thrilled with your product - it's a godsend - but must take exception to the misleading name. Would you be so kind as to get back to me on this subject matter? In the meantime, I'd be honored to recommend "Cat's Pride" to my friends !

Feline Fine,

Paul Rosa

Paul C. Rosa

410 North Michigan Avenue
Chicago, Illinois 60611
Phone 312-321-1515
Fax 312-321-1271

Cable Oil-Dri • Chicago, U.S.A.
Telex 910-221-5280

OIL•DRI

CORPORATION OF AMERICA

September 15, 1993

Mr. Paul C. Rosa
P.O. Box 9368
Colo. Springs, CO 80932

Dear Paul:

Thank you for the delightful letter about your cat (Jesse) and her appreciation of CAT'S PRIDE® cat litter. We are always pleased to hear from happy and satisfied customers...be it the cat or the owner. We at Oil-Dri would also like to thank your friend (Max), who recommended the product to you. We have enclosed free coupons as a token of our appreciation and, hopefully, you will also share them with Max. (Unfortunately, you did not state which product you used, so I have enclosed a variety of coupons).

I am also pleased to read that, finally, after ten years of dissatisfaction with other litters and your subsequent approval of CAT'S PRIDE®, you and your wife (Vicki) can now look forward to uninterrupted sound slumber and those reruns of...Matlock.

I am concerned, however, that you find the name **"CAT'S PRIDE®"** a bit odd. If you look up the word **"PRIDE"** in the dictionary, you will find the definition as such:

"Pleasure or satisfaction taken in one's work, achievements or possessions."

I am sure that after Jesse has "heaved and strained" in her box, the end result leaves her with a sense of satisfaction with her final achievement. With this definition in mind, I am sure the name **"CAT'S PRIDE®"** is quite suitable and hardly dishonest.

We'd like to thank you for your letter and hope that you will enjoy the enclosed coupons. We appreciate your continued support and recommendation of CAT'S PRIDE® to your friends.

Sincerely,

OIL-DRI CORPORATION OF AMERICA

Jayne M. Weiske
Product Manager
Consumer Products Division

JMW:jfk

(PR/JMW)

THE LEADER IN DEVELOPING, MANUFACTURING AND MARKETING SORBENT PRODUCTS...SINCE 1941

P.O. Box 9368
Colo. Springs, CO 80932
November 16, 1993

Jayne M. Weiske, Product Manager
Oil-Dri Corporation of America
410 North Michigan Ave.
Chicago, IL 60611

Dear Jayne (or "Ms. Weiske," if you insist!),

As you surely recall, I wrote to you on August 3, 1993, explaining that Cat's Pride Cat Litter was the first variety my cat (Jesse) found acceptable in ten years, After rejecting every other national brand with an insolent sniff, she embraced your product with all the enthusiasm she could muster! Even after writing you a congratulatory letter though, I remained somewhat skeptical, as Jesse puts the "ick" in finicky! But lo and behold, three months later she is still dutifully "unloading" into her litter box on a daily basis, and seems to have fully adopted Cat's Pride as her own. The experiment is definitely not a fluke, and I offer you (and yours) an unfettered salute!

Anyway, my friend, as I also mentioned earlier, Jesse's willingness to complete the excretory process without being let outside has allowed Vicki (my wife) and I to pursue...other interests. After several months of said pursuit, Vicki became pregnant (bless that E.P.T. Kit!), and we are eagerly awaiting our first child. As Cat's Pride is <u>directly</u> responsible for our now productive love life, we have chosen to name the child, "Jayne" or, if it's a boy, "Jay!" Yes, you've read correctly! So great is our devotion to you that we plan to include you (sort of) in the Rosa family. As I type, I am decorating my keyboard with tears of joy! Jayne, I've never felt so close to a stranger. What are *you* feeling?

Finally, I have a comment regarding the back of your Cat's Pride bags. It reads, "Cat's Pride: Why We're Proud." Then it goes on to explain why your <u>organization</u> is proud! Now, Jayne, you patiently (and effectively) convinced me in your first letter that cats can indeed be proud of their "performance," thus assuring me that the name, "Cat's Pride" was honest. But when I read the back of the bag, I am confused why you choose to explain the pride of the Oil-Dri Corporation rather than the pride of the thousands of lucky cats. It all seems so inconsistent and confusing! But since I feel comfortable enough to name my firstborn after you, I elected to write again to clear up this arduous matter.

Please contact me and let me know how you feel about our "tribute" to you, and explain the "back of the bag" question as well. Finally, if you have any (XL) Cat's Pride T-shirts, I'd love to have one. I would like to meet you, Jayne!!

Emotionally yours,

Paul Rosa

Paul C. Rosa

January 10, 1994

410 North Michigan Avenue
Chicago, Illinois 60611
Phone 312-321-1515
Fax 312-321-1271

Cable Oil-Dri • Chicago, U.S.A.
Telex 910-221-5280

Mr. Paul Rosa
P.O. Box 9368
Colo. Springs, CO 80932

Dear Paul (or Mr. Rosa, if preferred),

I apologize for the delay in responding to your letter, but work sometimes gets in the way of my job. It's a pleasure to hear that Jesse (your cat) is still dutifully "unloading" into her litter box and continues to support and appreciate the fine qualities of CAT'S PRIDE® Cat Litter. I guess you <u>can</u> teach an old cat new tricks!! Equally important, is the fact that your skepticism towards the performance of CAT'S PRIDE® has disappeared with each final (and proud) achievement that Jesse has left behind.

It was a delight to read that you and Vicki (your wife) are no longer being distracted during those episodes of Matlock and have been successful in pursuing...other interests. I am truly flattered that you have considered naming your firstborn after me. Unfortunately, while I also feel close to the Rosa family, I feel I must tell you that company policy discourages personal tributes of this kind. Instead, we recommend that all children conceived as a direct result of the success of CAT'S PRIDE®, be named after the product or even after the company's name. I am particularly fond of "Paul's Pride," that, while it might seem a bit long, could be shortened to P. P. Rosa. I find this alternative to be very descriptive of the product's attributes and an excellent tribute to you and the product name.

Mr. Rosa, I have significant concerns about your obsession with the text on the back of the CAT'S PRIDE® packaging. A recent market research study indicates that the majority of consumers do not read the back of the bag and therefore have little interest in what we place on it. After all, it's not as if the typical consumer places the package on the kitchen table and reads it as one does cereal packaging. I am concerned that you may be occasionally confusing our package with your Grape Nuts cereal. While CAT'S PRIDE® is a very fibrous product, I would not recommend that it be consumed on a regular basis. We have had reports of minor constipation associated with the accidental consumption of this product, particularly by humans.

Finally, as a gesture of Oil-Dri's appreciation of your new found loyalties (and obsession) with CAT'S PRIDE® , please accept the forthcoming CAT'S PRIDE® toy truck for your soon to arrive child. (We apologize that we are completely out of XL T-shirts.) Much continued success to you, Vicki (your wife) and Jesse (your cat) and P.P. (your forthcoming new family addition).

Sincerely,

OIL-DRI CORPORATION OF AMERICA

Jayne M. Weiske
Product Manager
Consumer Products Division

THE LEADER IN DEVELOPING, MANUFACTURING AND MARKETING SORBENT PRODUCTS...SINCE 1941

P.O. Box 9368
Colo. Springs, CO 80932
August 4, 1993

Customer Service
Colgate-Palmolive Company
New York, NY 10022

Dear Smile Maintainers,

I just finished watching a "Late Night with David Letterman" rerun and repaired to the bathroom to brush my teeth. After thoroughly scrubbing and rinsing, it occurred to me that I have been thrilled with your product (Regular Flavor Colgate Toothpaste) since I began using it in 1987. So I decided it was high time to write and say, "well done!"

Before I switched to Colgate I was literally a man without a toothpaste! I bounced around between Crest, Aim, Pepsodent, Aqua-Fresh, and even (gag!) generic brands. Nothing seemed to combine the *exact* great taste and fluoride protection I craved. I actually *dreaded* my (twice daily) trips to the sink!

Well, all that changed on February 18, 1987, when my mother (Kate) asked if I had tried Colgate. Amazingly, this was one of the only brands I had not tried, so I darted off to the neighborhood grocery store to buy a tube. In my excitement, I wrecked my car on the way, but that's another story. When I got home (by bus), I charged into the bathroom and "got to scrubbin'!" I was ecstatic; great taste and fluoride protection were mine at last! I'm *still* using the stuff, and can happily report *zero* cavities in six years. In fact, I'm so emotionally content now that I may just move out of my mother's house next year (after all, I *am* 37!). I suppose I can't give Colgate *all* the credit for my happiness, but good oral hygiene is the third most important thing in my life (after my mother and my cat, Vic).

Only one thing puzzles me. On the back of the tube appear the words, "FOR BEST RESULTS, SQUEEZE FROM THE BOTTOM AND FLATTEN IT AS YOU GO UP." I was a bit taken aback by this. What other choices are there? If you start at the *top* and flatten upward, nothing will happen. Would someone be dumb enough then to angrily throw the new tube away, crying foul? And wouldn't this same fool have trouble knowing which side is the bottom, rendering the above instructions useless anyway? I'd say so.

So, in conclusion, thanks for a terrific product. I plan to tell all my friends about it (I have many friends), and I've already convinced my mother to switch from Crest. But please get back to me on my question regarding the flattening instructions. It troubles me.

No fear of Dentists here,

Paul Rosa

Paul C. Rosa

P.S. If "four out of five dentists recommend sugarless gum for their patients who chew gum", what does the fifth one recommend, *pure sugar gum*?!

COLGATE-PALMOLIVE COMPANY
A Delaware Corporation

300 Park Avenue
New York, NY 10022-7499
Household Products
800-338-8388
Personal Care Products
800-221-4607

Consumer Affairs Department

August 26, 1993

Mr Paul Rosa
P.O. Box 9368
Colo. Springs, CO 80932

Dear Mr Rosa:

Thank you for your thoughtful comments about Colgate Great Regular Flavor Toothpaste. We are very pleased to learn that you enjoy using one of our products.

Our company has been a leading manufacturer for many years and has a well-earned reputation for offering quality products that meet consumer needs for convenience, value and outstanding performance. Still, it's always an added pleasure to receive compliments such as yours. You can be sure they will be shared with our company's management.

Regarding your question about flattening instructions, this statement was added when we switched to our current tube. Consumers liked to roll up the old aluminum tubes, but rolling doesn't work with the new plastic tubes.

We appreciate your taking the time to contact us. Please accept the enclosed with our compliments.

Sincerely,

Michele Morales

Michele Morales
Consumer Representative
Consumer Affairs

mmm/cl

Enclosures
0103379A

P.O. Box 9368
Colo. Springs, CO 80932
August 7, 1993

Customer Service
McDonald's - Corporate Headquarters
Oak Brook, IL 60521

Dear Burger Buddies,

I felt it was my responsibility to let you know how much your fine restaurants have meant to me over the years. I fell in love with McDonald's as a small lad of seven (in 1963), and the rest is history! Our family (I grew up in Pittsburgh) dined there once or twice a week, but when I left home for college, I decided to devote considerably more time to eating there. And did I ever!

Over the past twenty years, I have eaten at McDonald's over 15,500 times (I keep records)! That's an average of over two daily trips, and I'm proud of my consistency! My typical meal consists of two Big Macs, two Large Fries, an Apple Pie, and a Large Coke. I've eaten at McDonald's in all fifty states, but mostly in Pennsylvania, Virginia, and Colorado (my three homes so far). Have I set some sort of *frequency record*? Do you keep any such statistics? Am I entitled to some coupons or benefits, since I have spent approximately $70,000 on your food?

Anyway, since I am so fond of your organization, I thought I'd solicit some advice. Since high school, my weight has soared from 165 to 425 pounds. My cholesterol count has also crossed the 500 mark. The only exercise I get is walking to your restaurant - just a few blocks from my house. Would you recommend that I make fewer trips to McDonald's or is all the "healthy talk" just a load of rubbish? What do you suggest? I respect your advice, as you have brought me much joy over the years! Please respond soon!

McConcerned,

Paul Rosa

Paul C. Rosa

McDonald's Corporation
McDonald's Plaza
Oak Brook, Illinois 60521
Direct Dial Number

September 9, 1993

(708) 575-6198

Mr. Paul C. Rosa
P.O. Box 9368
Colo. Springs, CO 80932

Dear Mr. Rosa:

Thank you for being such a loyal McDonald's fan! We're delighted to know you've made 15,500+ visits to our restaurants. It's our pleasure to serve you.

While we don't keep any "frequency" records, we can safely tell you that you are definetly one of our most loyal customers. Also, since you are particularly fond of our Big Macs, you may be interested to know that the Big Mac celebrated its 25th year on the menu this year. We were proud to honor this sandwich, and its creator, Jim Dellagati, a McDonald's franchisee.

Regarding your diet, you may be interested to know that McDonald's menu can be a healthy part of any well-balanced diet. It's important to take your entire diet into consideration when you're planning your meals. Experts say, "balance, variety, and moderation" is the key to eating well.

To help you plan your meals with us, I've enclosed our "McDonald's Food Facts" and "McDonald's Today" brochures. These materials can educate on our food items' nutritional values and ingredients. Also, you may want to share these materials with a health professional for dietary advice.

Mr. Rosa, in appreciation of your dedication to the Golden Arches, I've enclosed our "Certificate of Good Taste," and some gift certificates. We thank you again for being a McDonald's customer, and look forward to serving you for many years to come.

Sincerely,

McDONALD'S CORPORATION

Julie Cleary, Representative
Customer Satisfaction Department

Enclosures: "McDonald's Food Facts" & "McDonald's Today"
"Certificate of Good Taste" & gift certificates

P.O. Box 9368
Colo. Springs, CO 80932
August 7, 1993

Imodium A-D Anti-Diarrheal
McNeil Consumer Products Co.
Division of McNeil-PPC, Inc.
Fort Washington, PA 19034

Dear Bathroom Advisors,

Last month I had a bout of diarrhea that was not to be believed! Over the course of two days I rushed to the "facilities" at least thirty-five times, and felt as drained as a Municipal Pool in autumn. So complete was my woe, that I feared my internal organs would start splashing into the bowl next. Imagine the horror!

Finally, I struggled to the pharmacy and picked up a bottle of Imodium A-D (I've seen your fine commercials on TV). When I got home, I promptly ingested eight teaspoons and (skeptically) waited for the flood gates to close. And close they did!

Over the past eighteen days, I haven't had a call from nature even once! The flood gates have not only closed, they've apparently been *padlocked*! It's frightening, I tell you. My appetite is healthy, but nothing is "exiting the premises!" I'm becoming concerned - will I have an internal eruption if this condition does not soon dissipate? I am deathly afraid of physicians, and don't know where to turn. Would you please drop me a line quickly (I have no phone)? What's in that Imodium A-D, cement?!

All Plugged Up,

Paul Rosa

Paul C. Rosa

P.S. Do you have any merchandise for sale (clothing, caps, etc.)?

McNEIL

McNEIL CONSUMER PRODUCTS COMPANY, 7050 CAMP HILL ROAD, FORT WASHINGTON, PA 19034 (215) 233-7000

August 24, 1993

Mr. Paul C. Rosa
P.O. Box 9368
Colo. Springs, CO 80932

Dear Mr. Rosa:

Although we were sorry to learn of your dissatisfaction with our IMODIUM® A-D (loperamide HCl) Anti-Diarrheal Liquid, we appreciate that you have taken the time to write.

IMODIUM A-D products are safe and effective for the relief of acute nonspecific diarrhea, including Travelers' Diarrhea, when taken according to directions on the package label.

Please note, the package label of this product states, "Take four teaspoonfuls after the first loose bowel movement, followed by two teaspoonfuls after each subsequent loose bowel movement, but no more than eight teaspoonfuls a day for no more than two days."

In certain instances, when a patient has the occasion to take a product for an illness, symptoms associated with the illness or a coincidental medical condition may be mistaken for side effects of the medication. Good medical practice dictates that you consult your physician about any health concerns you may have, as your physician is familiar with you and your personal medical history.

Additionally, for your reference, McNeil CPC markets primarily over-the-counter medications; we do not have clothing or caps for sale. We take great pride in our product quality and customer satisfaction; therefore, enclosed is a check to cover your purchase price and postage.

Sincerely,

Denise M. Hunt

Denise M. Hunt, RPh
Medical Information Specialist

DMH/cl
0170758A

T-shirt Received

Enc: check

P.O. Box 9368
Colo. Springs, CO 80932
August 9, 1993

Customer Service
M & M's Candies
Division of Mars, Inc.
Hackettstown, N.J. 07840

Dear Chocolate Champions,

I have been stuffing my face with your delicious chocolates since I was a small boy!
They bring great joy to my life, and I often grieve for the unfortunate folks in the world
who don't have access to tasty, sugary treats! I can't imagine life without them (the
treats). I had also enjoyed your clever M & M's slogan ("It melts in your mouth, not in
your hands!") for as long as I could remember...but all that changed several months ago.

While vacationing in Alaska last February, I was the victim of a brutal grizzly bear attack.
I was foolish enough to go hiking with several jars of honey in my knapsack (I'm a honey
nut!), and it cost me my left arm and 30% of my scalp. But as a devout Lutheran, I
realized God was generous enough to let me escape with my life!

Anyway, soon afterward I began to think about your slogan, "It melts in your mouth, not
in your **hands**!" I realized this no longer applied to me, as one of my hands was now
gone, and I grew depressed. I suppose I had been insensitive to the handicapped before,
as it never occurred to me that this was truly prejudicial! What about the feelings of those
with just one hand? Or *no* hands? They like candy too, for heaven's sake!

So I came up with a (slightly!) new M & M's slogan for you: "It melts in your mouth,
not in your hand(s)...if you have any!" Admittedly, this is a bit wordy, but it would be
politically correct, and consider the feelings of *everyone*. I would be willing to sign the
necessary documents to give full credit for this slogan to Mars, Inc. Sure, I could demand
compensation, but I'm pleased to contribute to the goodwill of mankind!

Please write and let me know what you think of my idea. Also, if you have merchandise
(T-shirts, sweatshirts, ascots, etc.) for sale, let me know! Thank you, and god bless!

Chocolate is life,

Paul Rosa

Paul C. Rosa

P.O. Box 9368
Colo. Springs, CO 80932
September 23, 1993

Customer Service
M & M's Candies
Division of Mars, Inc.
Hackettstown, N.J. 07840

Dear Candy Characters,

Well, it's been six weeks since I wrote, and I'm beginning to think a response simply isn't coming! After serving my country for **38 years** in the Navy, I blithely assumed that I would be treated with dignity and respect during my golden years. Then along comes Mars, Inc., and my assumption is shattered!

And then it occurred to me: "Maybe they're not responding because I'm handicapped, and *that* makes them uncomfortable!" As a survivor of two wars *and* a grizzly bear attack, I *demand* to be treated with the civility I have coming to me! I simply will not be dismissed as a "war horse" or "cripple," damn it!

With this in mind, I am patiently re-submitting my original letter, and displaying my suggested (politically correct) M & M's logo here:

"It melts in your mouth, not in your hand(s)...if you have any!"

I would appreciate a little courtesy this time, folks, and not have my letter tossed aside as a "consumer nuisance!" I look forward to a *swift* reply. Thank you and god bless.

Handing it to you,

Paul Rosa

Paul C. Rosa

P.S. Please send a (XL) T-shirt.

P.O. Box 9368
Colo. Springs, CO 80932
October 22, 1993

Mr. William Hellegas, President
M & M's Candies
Division of Mars, Inc.
High Street
Hackettstown, N.J. 07840

Dear Mr. Hellegas,

It pains me to disturb the busy president of a major corporation, but when the customer service department proves slothful or delinquent, it is my custom to go to the top banana (if you will). On August 9, 1993 I diligently wrote to M & M's Candies, explaining that I recently lost my left arm in a brutal grizzly bear attack. Now I'm not one who seeks any sympathy whatsoever, but I certainly am more sensitive to the handicapped now. You've heard that expression, "walk a mile in someone else's shoes," ...or something like that.

As a voracious M & M's eater -I've gorged myself on them since I was a playful squirt in Clarion, PA (pop. 43,362)- the motto, "It melts in your mouth not in your hands," has lately became more and more objectionable. You see, sir, as a one-armed (and consequently one-handed) man, this advertisement doesn't even acknowledge me as a potential customer. Again, I'm not a whiner or complainer -38 years in the Navy exorcised all signs of these traits- but I don't sit still when my feelings are trampled on! You see, Mr. Hellegas, I am a fiercely proud man.

When I proposed a new slogan for M & M's **("It melts in your mouth, not in your hand(s)...if you have any!")** my correspondence was never answered. I re-submitted my letter on September 23, 1993, and have now waited a total of ten weeks without a response. Is this any way to treat a Korean War veteran? I think not.

I knew that I would be treated with dignity if I wrote to the president (you). Respect for the consumer is a characteristic that helped pave your way to the top, no doubt! Again, I apologize for the intrusion, but it seems I have no other recourse. I am enclosing my two initial letters, and urge *you* to finally respond to my suggestion. I am not looking for blind agreement, simply a discussion of my point. A self-addressed, stamped envelope (SASE) is also enclosed for your convenience. Thank you and God bless!

What's the deal with the green M & M's?

Paul Rosa

Paul C. Rosa

a division of Mars, Incorporated
High Street, Hackettstown, New Jersey 07840 ● Telephone 908-852-1000

November 24, 1993

Mr. Paul C. Rosa
P.O. Box 9368
Colo. Springs, CO 80932

Dear Mr. Rosa:

Thank you for your most recent letter addressed to Mr. Hellegas and
forwarded to me for response.

As you can imagine, we receive thousands of letters offering
suggestions and ideas to improve our products as well as our
advertising. Our advertising is not directed towards a specific group
of people but rather to the general public. We apologize if we have
offended you in any way; we certainly did not intend to do so.

Thank you again for writing. Please remain our valued consumer and
accept the enclosed store coupons for a treat with our compliments.

Sincerely,

Marilyn Womer

Marilyn Womer
Consumer Affairs

MEW/cl 0251264A

P.O. Box 9368
Colo. Springs, CO 80932
August 9, 1993

Customer Service
e • p • t (Early Pregnancy Test)
Parke - Davis
Consumer Health Products Group
Morris Plains, NJ 07950

Dear Fetal Folks,

I would like to thank you for your superb product! For years, my girlfriend has used e.p.t., and the results have been consistently accurate: "Negative!" Yahoo!

My girlfriend (Agnes) and I decided years ago that we shouldn't reproduce. You see, she is a heavy drinker, and I have a violent temper, so we use an *incredible* combination of birth control methods (diaphragm, birth control pills, condom, and early withdrawal, all at once!). Then your product rewards our diligence with a reassuring response. "Hats off to you!" I say.

I also enjoy your TV commercials, but feel they unfairly target a select percentage of the population. All of them address one of the two following situations:

      A. A positive test result makes the couple happy, or
      B. A negative test result upsets the couple.

Well, that covers *some* people, but what about the remainder:

      C. A positive test result upsets the couple, or
      D. A negative result makes the couple happy (US!).

As these possibilities comprise *at least* 50% of all couples, I feel it would be responsible to show such commercials! My girlfriend and I have some high school acting experience, so we'd be happy to contribute. It could go something like this:

      AGNES (calls from bathroom): It's negative! I am NOT pregnant!!
      PAUL: Really?! That's FANTASTIC!!! (We dance about).

So, folks, I think it's high time to show more truth in advertising. Please write and let me know what you think of my idea. I look forward to your reply.

Ovary well,

Paul Rosa

Paul C. Rosa

October 7, 1993

WARNER LAMBERT

Paul C. Rosa
P.O. Box 9368
Colo. Springs, CO 80932

Dear Mr. Rosa:

Thank you for your interest in e·p·t advertising. I have attached a copy of an article which answers some of your questions about our advertising campaign.

Enclosed please find an informational brochure on e·p·t for your future reference. We are pleased to have you as a valued customer.

Sincerely,

Warner-Lambert
Customer Service

P.O. Box 9368
Colo. Springs, CO 80932
August 10, 1993

Consumer Affairs
Preparation H
Whitehall Laboratories, Inc.
New York, NY 10017

Dear Hemorrhoid Honchos,

I'm writing to tell you that your product has turned a desperate man into one who can't stop whistling! It all began in April of this year when I developed what I thought was a small pimple...down there. I thought little of it, but it began to grow, and by the end of May it had reached the volume of a Ping-Pong ball! Yes, I was concerned, but as I have a dread of physicians that is all-consuming, I refused to act. And it got worse! By mid June this seemingly innocent pimple had reached the dimensions of a billiard ball! Sleeping was now difficult, and sitting comfortably was simply out of the question (excruciating!). I actually had a *standing* desk installed in my office, telling my co-workers that I wanted "more exercise." I couldn't drive safely to work, so I took cabs, tilting awkwardly in the back seat, so as not to torment my delicate hindquarters. By July, the offending lump had swelled to the size of a softball, and I could no longer conceal it beneath clothing, so I quit my job and became a recluse. Trapped in my own home, I had the necessities delivered while I contemplated ending it all. Then, two weeks ago, fate stepped in!

As I was watching a hysterical episode of "Designing Women" (they're *sassy*, don't you think?), I saw your fine commercial. The skilled actor delivered the lines that saved my life: "My doctor said my condition wouldn't need surgery, and suggested I use Preparation H!" Well, let me tell you, I almost jumped through the ceiling with joy (I was already standing, as I hadn't used a chair in weeks!). I rushed to the corner pharmacy - my first venture outside in ages - and purchased a tube of this "magic stuff." For the past few weeks I have religiously lathered the "atrocity" with your soothing ointment, and to my delight, have witnessed a miracle. After five days, the "softball" had returned to "Ping-Pong" status, and the (cautious) bounce returned to my step. After three more days, the little devil was the size of a cashew, and I began to sing catchy tunes (i.e. "Cherokee Nation" by Paul Revere and the Raiders). Today the hemorrhoid is no more than a speck, and my old, upbeat attitude is here to stay. In the past few weeks I've gotten my job back and I've started dating a lovely young woman (Claire). Without your terrific product and succinct commercials I would have been dead by now (and unable to compose this letter, naturally). "Thank you!" really isn't saying enough.

Finally, do you keep any statistics on hemorrhoid sizes? Have I set a record? I certainly wouldn't be proud of this distinction, but it *is* of interest to me! Please write to me and let me know! Also, do you have any merchandise for sale? I'd be happy to advertise Preparation H on the front of my T-shirt or ball cap! I look forward to your speedy response! God bless Whitehall Laboratories!!!

Swell no more,

Paul Rosa

Paul C. Rosa

P.S. I have photographs to confirm my potential record. Shall I send them?

P.O. Box 9368
Colo. Springs, CO 80932
September 27, 1993

Consumer Affairs
Preparation H
Whitehall Laboratories, Inc.
New York, NY 10017

Dear Medical Marvels,

Perhaps I owe you an apology. I wrote a letter (August 10) detailing the rise and fall of my incredible hemorrhoid. I thought it was well stated at the time, but, with the benefit of hindsight, I realize it was a bit...graphic. As you recall, I explained that it had grown as large as a softball (at its zenith) before Preparation H saved the day. I apologize for the "direct" approach I used, but you must understand that I was raised by a simple rancher in Jasper, AR (pop. 519), and that's the only way he knew! Several tours of duty in Vietnam certainly did nothing to soften my approach.

You may also remember that I asked if my hemorrhoid had "set a record." Again, this was probably a bit crude, but I am soon contacting Ripley's Believe It or Not, hoping for a lucrative deal. That's why I urgently need to know if you've ever heard of more advanced swelling than what I experienced. If I am indeed the record holder **and** Ripley's rewards me with a contract, my niece, Agnes, has a chance to attend college (UCLA or Chatham College in Pittsburgh). Frankly, I don't make much money as a forklift operator (I quit my desk job at AAA), and the Ripley's money could do much good for my family!

My girlfriend (Claire) encouraged me to re-submit my original letter and apologize for its explicit wording, but also to politely ask you to pass on any "hemorrhoid size statistics" you may keep. If I haven't offended you too much, I'd certainly appreciate a response, my friends! It would mean a lot to me. Also, a (XL) T-shirt would be a cherished (though admittedly unusual) gift. Do you have any? I look forward to a *swift* reply.

Apologetically yours,

Paul Rosa

Paul C. Rosa (Veteran)

P.S. Claire and I are to be wed next April (details to follow)!

Anthony J. Ewell, PhD
Director, Drug Surveillance &
Medical Information

Whitehall-Robins
5 Giralda Farms
Madison, NJ 07940-0871
Telephone (201) 660-5830

WHITEHALL ROBINS

December 7, 1993

Mr. Paul C. Rosa
P.O. Box 9368
Colo. Springs, CO 80932

REFERENCE: PREPARATION® H

Dear Mr. Rosa

Thank you very much for your letter and your endorsement of Preparation H. We have carefully considered your request for information regarding size of hemorrhoids that have been reported to us. Unfortunately, all medical information that we obtain is confidential. Therefore, we really cannot be of assistance to you with regard to you contacting Ripley's.

We appreciate your interest in our products.

Very truly yours,

[signature: Anthony J. Ewell]

ll Ph.D.

WHITEHALL ROBINS

Whitehall-Robins
5 Giralda Farms
Madison, NJ 07940-0871
Telephone (201) 660-5500

December 8, 1993

Mr. Paul Rosa
P.O. Box 9368
Colo. Springs, CO 80932

Dear Mr. Rosa:

This is in response to your letters of Preparation H on August 10 and September 27, 1993.

We do not have statistics on the size of hemorrhoids. We, also, do not have promotional tee-shirts or other Preparation H items. We are pleased that you received such positive results from our product.

We appreciate your taking the time to write about your positive experience. Under separate cover, we are sending you a sample with our compliments. Please allow 2-3 weeks for delivery.

Sincerely,

[signature: Cecelia McDonnell]

Cecelia McDonnell
Manager, Consumer Affairs

P.O. Box 9368
Colo. Springs, CO 80932
August 14, 1993

Consumer Affairs
Rand McNally & Company
P.O. Box 7600
Chicago, IL 60680

Dear Map Makers,

I thought I'd drop you a line to let you know how much your fine maps and atlases have meant to me over the years! Since I was a small boy growing up in north-central West Virginia, my family and I have enjoyed the many benefits of your accurate, descriptive products. I congratulate your terrific firm (North America's best)!

Now I am a full grown man of forty-seven, using the "Rand McNally Road Atlas (Gift Edition)." As a salesman of fine Llama collars and feeding troughs, I spend approximately thirty-five weeks a year on the road, peddling my wares at farms and zoos. Many times I have driven 500 miles in one day, keeping difficult appointments with the help of your pinpoint maps!

Yes, I have always been impressed with your unfailing accuracy, but have had trouble with one feature which you consistently depict. Your atlas shows that states have *lines* which separate them from other states, forming borders. Many times I have driven from one state to the next, but I can never find the lines, no matter how hard I look! I realize that they may be old and faded, or buried beneath grass and other debris, but it's amazing that I have never spotted even a few yards of these "dividers!"

Several days ago, I traveled on Route 50 to Garden City, Kansas (where I landed a lucrative Llama contract). On the way, I spent over ninety minutes searching for the *elusive* line near Holly, Colorado (pop. 969), at the Colorado/Kansas border. My son (Leo) and I finally grew disgusted and sped off, somewhat disappointed in your company. If these lines truly *do* exist, as your maps "promise", where on earth (no pun intended) are they? Leo *also* pointed out that they may be intentionally buried, so as not to distract motorists. He *is* a clever fellow, and it's as good an explanation as I've heard, but I remain unconvinced. You don't print other buried items (electrical lines, etc.) on your maps, so what gives?! As a faithful consumer, I would appreciate a quick, concise reply. It would certainly comfort me. Aside from the above troublesome issue, keep up the good work, my friends!

On the road again,

Paul Rosa

Paul C. Rosa

**RAND MCNALLY**

8255 North Central Park
Skokie IL 60076-2970

708·329·8100
Cable: RANALLY Skokie IL
Mail to: Box 7600
Chicago IL 60680-9913

"Our 137th Year"
September 22, 1993

Mr. Paul C. Rosa
P.O. Box 9368
Colo. Springs, CO 80932

Dear Mr. Rosa,

Thank you for your letter about the <u>Rand McNally Road Atlas: United States / Canada / Mexico</u>. The lines for state boundaries are only map representations of the state borders and are not physically present. Sometimes along an interstate or highway there is a sign that indicates that you are now entering an adjoining state, but there are no lines.

We appreciate you taking the time to write.

Sincerely,

Janet Pawlowski

Janet Pawlowski
Public Relations

P.O. Box 9368
Colo. Springs, CO 80932
August 18, 1993

Management
The Big Texan Restaurant
7700 E. Interstate 40
Amarillo, TX 79112

Dear Steak Lovers,

As a frequent traveler to Amarillo (I am a salesman of quality scarves and Windbreakers),
I usually take time to visit your fine restaurant. I have been consistently intrigued with
your 72 ounce steak challenge - If you finish it in one hour you get it free! I have seen the
"wall of fame," with the list of those brave souls who have successfully tackled the
behemoth hunk of meat. I was also told by an employee that one man actually ate two
steaks (nine pounds!!), setting a consumption record.

Well my friends, after years of "training," I believe that I can polish off THREE steaks
(216 oz.!!) within the one hour time limit. I know this is probably unprecedented, but as I
carry 625 pounds on my six foot, nine inch frame, it's within my grasp! Before I cruise
down there and smash the record, I want to be *certain* that this has *never* been done
before. I also want the following concerns addressed:

- Is it permissible to eat with one's bare hands (it's quicker)?
- Would I receive some sort of cash reward/city parade?
- How much would it cost me if I fail?
- How many calories is that? Am I putting my heart at immediate risk?
- Can I bring my own seasonings?

Since I am willing to tackle something that's probably never been done, I obviously want
to know exactly what I'm getting into. Please get back to me on the above issues as soon
as possible, so I can make my plans! Then prepare to be amazed!

Step aside wimps,

Paul Rosa

Paul C. Rosa

P.O. Box 9368
Colo. Springs, CO 80932
September 1, 1993

Mr. Bob Lee
The Big Texan Restaurant
7700 E. Interstate 40
Amarillo, TX 79112

Dear Bob,

I received your recent message on my answering machine, stating your desire to discuss my outrageous claim that I can devour 13.5 pounds of steak! I appreciate the swift response to my letter (and the use of your toll free number), but there are certain reasons why I wish to correspond only by mail - for now. Allow me to explain.

As I assume this has never been done before - and maybe never again! - I feel it adds an important element of mystery to the event if I remain somewhat secretive. I have explained that I am an enormous salesman, but choose to reveal little else about myself. Certain potential endorsement deals may follow a successful attempt (A-1 Steak Sauce, Heinz Catsup, etc.), and I don't want to hurt my chances by telling too much before I need to!

With this in mind, I urge you to address the questions posed in my letter of August 18, 1993. If you no longer have the letter, I am re-submitting it for your convenience, my friend. I think it will be best for all concerned if this event has an air of great anticipation about it! I'm sure you can appreciate my delicate circumstances! I look forward to your expedient, *written* reply! Thanks so much!

Pass the Tums,

Paul Rosa

Paul C. Rosa

BIG TIME BIG TEXAN

☆ BIG BOB LEE ☆

9-3-93

I talked with Commissioner Rick Perry from the Department of Agriculture, And he is very exicted. He has the wheels turning on Capitol hill in Austin.

Affiliated foods has committed A major sponsorship and has been in contact with A 1 steak sauce, I do not know to what extent, but As soon As I find out I will let you know.

Needless to say this event will get national exposure And the opport- unities for All envolved Are limitless

We will keep you posted, And look forward to A great event

☆

Bulletin board

Up in Colorado Springs there lives a man who a) does not have all his oars in the water; b) has an appetite that would stagger an elephant; or c) is enjoying a vast practical joke. And **Bob Lee** at the Big Texan is eager to meet him and find out which it is. Bob has a letter from the man, Paul C. Rosa, in which Rosa says he's visited Amarillo several times and is intrigued by the Big Texan's famed 72-ounce steak challenge. Rosa says polishing off one steak dinner with trimmings is no big deal. He isn't even awed by the 1965 feat of **Klondike Bill**, described by the Globe-Times of that day as a popular local wrestler, who wolfed down two complete meals. Rosa proclaims himself ready to put away three. ''As I carry 625 pounds on my 6-foot, 9-inch frame, it's within my grasp!'' he writes. He closes the letter, ''Step aside, wimps.''

Just out of curiosity, we tried to calculate the calories involved in this enterprise, using the Encyclopedia of Food Values. A shrimp cocktail would be about 113; a 72-ounce steak maybe 5,490; a small baked potato with skin, 124; a dinner roll, 50, a salad 12, and toss in some Italian salad dressing and a couple pats of butter for about 300. Now, multiply all that by three and Mr. Rosa would be packing in about 18,267 calories, give or take a few hundred. **Sharon Fischer**, High Plains Baptist Hospital dietitian, was more conservative, calculating that the steak would lose a quarter of its mass in cooking. She pegged the grand total at about 13,500. But who's counting?

Bob, who can spot a promotional opportunity like a hawk spies a field mouse, promises to let us know when the great event is scheduled to occur.

Almanac: On this date in 1951, the TV soap opera ''Search for Tomorrow'' made its debut on CBS.

Cathy Martindale
Executive Editor

**from the
Amarillo Globe Times**

P.O. Box 9368
Colo. Springs, CO 80932
August 19, 1993

Consumer Affairs
Johnson & Johnson Co.
Dental Floss Division
New Brunswick, NJ 08903

Dear Food Finders,

Your product is, quite simply, the best on the market, bar none! I've flossed with Johnson & Johnson Dentotape (Waxed) Ribbon Floss since an embarrassing incident in 1980. You see, I was the valedictorian at my high school, and as I gave the commencement address, the front rows began to giggle. "Oh my god! My fly must be open!" I thought, as I stole a glance downward. Much to my relief, this was not the case, and my speech continued. The giggling continued as well, and it was soon apparent that a large chunk of food (pasta) was lodged between my two front teeth. Although I removed the offending particle with my tongue and the speech was well received, the incident haunts me to this day. I vowed never to leave clean teeth and gums to chance again. And I never have!

Since that day, I have religiously flossed with your product two times a day, and have received numerous compliments on my smile. Last year, a young woman (a stranger) on the bus commented, "You have a nice smile." Well, we are engaged to be wed this December, believe it or not! So, your dental floss has really helped me become more confident and successful (I'm a Vascular Surgeon). But recently my trust in Johnson & Johnson took a dreadful turn.

I buy the 100 yard roll of floss and have never doubted that I was getting that much. However, recently I began to have doubts. You see, I always use _**exactly**_ ten inches of floss, as this provides the best results without waste. At ten inches per flossing (twice daily), a roll should last **180 days** (100 yards = 300 feet = 3600 inches ÷ 10 inches = 360 flossings ÷ 2 [a day] = **180 days**). Well, on August 5, 1992 I bought a 100 yard roll and was dismayed to run out of floss *172 days* later - January 24, 1993! I thought this was just a fluke, and began using a new roll the following day. *168 days* later - July 12, last month - I was enraged when the spool ran out!

"How many yards of dental floss does Johnson & Johnson owe me?!" I asked myself. In these two examples, the answer is 400 inches total (11.11 yards, damn it!). I know that's not exactly draining my savings account, but it's the principle that matters! Perhaps your company thinks a few yards here and there won't make any difference to the consumer, but will *save* a few precious bucks! Well, I won't buy into this atrocity! As of July 13, I've switched brands of dental floss, and have suggested that the hospital where I work do the same (that's a *lot* of floss!). But then I decided to write and give you a chance to defend yourselves. As your company has been consistently impressive to me, I figured it was the least I could do.

Please write and let me know your thoughts on my above "accusations." And please don't suggest that *my* calculations are off - I'm a surgeon, remember? I anxiously await your reply.

⊗ Fightin' mad,

Paul Rosa

Paul C. Rosa, M.D.

P.O. Box 9368
Colo. Springs, CO 80932
October 2, 1993

Consumer Affairs
Johnson & Johnson Co.
Dental Floss Division
New Brunswick, NJ 08903

Dear Mouth Mavericks,

As a vascular surgeon with very little time to spare, I am extremely disappointed that my letter of August 19, 1993 was never answered. With my busy schedule of surgery and university lectures, I like to spend my free time with my family (my wife, Kate, and my kids Naomi, Rubi, and Ned), not writing follow-up letters to apathetic corporations! But as a thirteen-year user of Johnson & Johnson Dental Floss, I feel I've earned the right to a prompt, courteous reply. Since the "prompt" part is no longer possible, perhaps you can come through with the "courteous" part.

Kate encouraged me to re-submit my original letter, suggesting, "It was probably lost in the mail room." Ah, sweet, forgiving Kate! She'd probably find a way to exonerate Jeffrey Dahmer! But I *am* including a copy of my first letter, and aggressively requesting that it is (finally!) addressed. Again, I complained that your "100 yard roll" of floss contained considerably less than advertised in two *separate* studies! How thorough is the testing of the floss length? Perhaps the attitude is, "95 yards, 100 yards, what's the difference?" Well, there's a big difference, my friends! Hard-working Americans deserve so much more!

On a peculiar note, I have a (shy) friend, Kurt, who recently lost an arm in a nasty Grizzly Bear encounter. He has been unable to floss since, and wanted me to ask you if there are any devices available for one-armed flossing. I look forward to a swift reply on all of the above issues, and hope a reunion with Johnson & Johnson is in my future! God bless.

Feeling slighted,

Paul Rosa

Paul C. Rosa, M.D.

P.S. Please send a (XL) T-shirt.

December 13, 1993

Dr. Paul Rosa
P.O. Box 9368
Colo. Springs, CO 80932

Dear Dr. Rosa:

Thank you again for contacting Johnson & Johnson Consumer Products, Inc. Your most recent letter, along with copies of your previous correspondence, has been forwarded to my attention. We apologize for the delay in responding to you. We had hoped to have the opportunity to speak with you personally.

Johnson & Johnson has produced dental floss for many years according to the highest standards and specifications. Each container of floss is wound and packaged under strictly monitored conditions. Despite the many steps incorporated in the manufacturing process to ensure accuracy in filling, your packages were apparently not up to the high standards consumers have every right to expect from our company. We apologize for the inconvenince and have forwarded your comments on to the appropriate personnel.

You stated in your letter that you use ten inches each time you floss your teeth. Our research indicates that eighteen inches of floss is the optimum amount to use per cleaning. Enclosed is a brochure with information about flossing that may be of interest to you.

Also enclosed is a brochure and samples of our STIM-U-DENT* Plaque Removers, which your friend who cannot floss might find beneficial. STIM-U-DENT* Plaque Removers are specially shaped basswood sticks used to clean between the teeth like floss. Many people who find flossing difficult have discovered using STIM-U-DENT* Plaque Removers to be a convenient and effective alternative to flossing. STIM-U-DENT* is

Page 2
December 13, 1993
Dr. Rosa

recognized by the American Dental Association and recommended by many dentists for patients who find flossing difficult or impossible.

We regret that we do not have the T-Shirt you requested, but we hope that you find the enclosed information and samples of use. Again, thank you for your interest in Johnson & Johnson Consumer Products, Inc.

Sincerely,

Janet L. Ward
Manager

1263528B
*Trademark
Enclosures

P.O. Box 9368
Colo. Springs, CO 80932
August 21, 1993

Consumer Affairs
Beiersdorf, Inc.
Nivea Ultra Moisturizing Creme
Norwalk, CT 06856-5529

Dear Moisture Mavens,

Since 1963, when I was a high school student in Florence, SC, I've used your terrific moisturizing creme (cream?) to keep my skin youthful and vibrant. For a long time I used it only on my face, but in 1978 (as a thirty-two-year-old) I decided to commit myself to fighting the aging process with a vengeance! As *today* is the fifteen year anniversary of my unusual "endeavor," I decided to finally share it with you!

On August 21, 1978, as I began noticing the inevitable effects of father time on my skin, I undertook a remarkable (perhaps peculiar) experiment. I fashioned a large (2' x 3' x 7') box out of plywood, installed a waterproof liner, and proceeded to "ladle" in **1,500 jars** of Nivea Creme - that's **9,000 ounces**! Since that day, I've slept naked in this box every night (except when I occasionally travel), immersing myself completely to the neck in creme. I also still smear a generous portion on my face. Once a month I shovel out the old creme (it begins to smell rancid), and replace it completely. Then I plunge in again - yahoo! It is fantastically warm and comfortable!

Now, before you write me off as a raving lunatic, allow me to share the results. I am convinced that my skin has not aged *one day* in fifteen years! It is incredibly smooth and silky, almost luxurious to the touch! I am now forty-seven years old, but people I meet don't believe that. Even after seeing my driver's license birth date, they think it's been altered - I *still* look like a man in his early thirties! I'd be happy to send you photographs, because I think I've found the fountain of youth!!!

But you may wonder about the social consequences. Admittedly, I shared my bed with no one until I met my fiancee ("Ruth Anne"). But after her initial reservations, she "took the plunge" with me, and was delighted with the way it made her feel (the *sex* was unbelievable as well!). When we get married next year, we plan to build an enormous (**15,000 ounce**) sleeping box. Based on past results, our love may truly be "eternal!" Perhaps we will teach our children to sleep in "Creme Boxes" as well!

So, have you ever heard of such a thing? Do *you* ever encourage folks to submerge their persons completely in Nivea? As I spend approximately $3,000 a month on your product (I'm a wealthy lawyer), I was also wondering if I qualify for a discount. And do you have any use for "old" Nivea? It seems like such a waste to discard it just because it's a bit smelly. I could ship it to you every month. I look forward to your reply, my lifelong friends! Oh yeah, Ruth Anne says, "Hi!"

Agelessly yours,

Paul Rosa

Paul C. Rosa, Attorney at Law

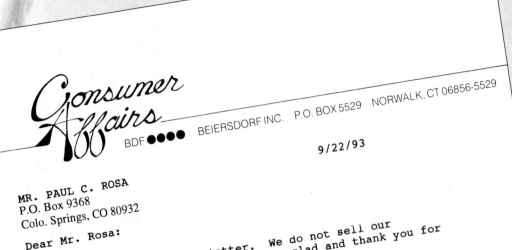

Consumer Affairs

BDF ●●●● BEIERSDORF INC. P.O. BOX 5529 NORWALK, CT 06856-5529

9/22/93

MR. PAUL C. ROSA
P.O. Box 9368
Colo. Springs, CO 80932

Dear Mr. Rosa:

Thank you for your recent letter. We do not sell our products direct to consumers. We are glad and thank you for using our Nivea Creme.

Agian thank you for your letter. We hope you will continue to use Beiersdorf's fine line of skin care products.

Sincerely,

Paul Smith
Consumer Affairs Administrator

P.O. Box 9368
Colo. Springs, CO 80932
September 27, 1993

Mr. Paul Smith
Consumer Affairs Administrator
Beiersdorf, Inc.
P.O. Box 5529
Norwalk, CT 06856-5529

Dear Mr. Smith (Is "Paul" too forward?),

Thank you kindly for the swift response to my letter of August 21, 1993. Concern for the customer is what will eventually return American businesses to their rightful positions (near the top!) in the world community. Nivea continues to set the standard for moisturizers!

I was troubled to hear that you do not sell products directly to the consumer, as I am tired of spending $3,000 a month at the local store. You failed to tell me if old Nivea Creme is of any use, or if "sleeping submerged in Nivea" is a familiar practice to Beiersdorf. I assume (by your silence) that both answers are, "no." Since I am surely one of your best customers, I hoped my letter would be conscientiously addressed. Don't you think that's fair? This former Marine certainly does!

I was also disappointed by the grammar in your (painfully short) letter. I've enclosed a copy of your note and marked the "trouble areas." Of the five sentences, two (**fully 40%**) have errors! The third sentence ("We are glad and thank you for using our Nivea Creme.") is so woeful that it would take half a page to criticize it thoroughly! The first sentence (fourth overall) in the second paragraph contains the word, "again," spelled, "a-g-i-a-n!" That's atrocious, and I consider it a slap in the face! Paul (good name!), I don't want to be picky, but as a Consumer Affairs Administrator, isn't good grammar *vital*? Aren't you putting your job in jeopardy when you send such sorry letters?

As a big supporter (what an understatement!) of Beiersdorf, Inc., I feel I've earned the right to receive *thorough* responses, written in crisp English. Granted, I *am* a very meticulous attorney, but I don't think I'm asking for too much! Please attempt to answer future questions (from all customers, not just me!) in a concise fashion, Paul! Finally, Ruth Anne says, "Hi!" again.

Still taking the plunge,

Paul Rosa

Paul C. Rosa, Attorney at Law

P.S. Please send a (XL) T-shirt.
P.P.S. Why is it spelled c-r-e-m-e?

No Further Response!

P.O. Box 9368
Colo. Springs, CO 80932
August 22, 1993

Consumer Affairs
Uncle Ben's, Inc.
P.O. Box 1752
Houston, TX 77251

Dear Taste Bud Tempters,

Let's face it, I *love* rice. I *have* always loved rice, and damn it, I *will* always love rice! It tastes good with everything: fish, chicken, pork, steak, ham, even SPAM! Everything! I've been eating rice for as long as I can remember, and I'm convinced that it's the greatest food *ever*! Rice has been such an important part of my life, that in Uncle Ben's honor, I plan to attend Rice University in Houston next year (I trust there's an affiliation). I will study Food Services, and hope to one day work for your organization across town! As I currently carry a 4.0 grade average, I feel my chances are good. Do you offer summer intern programs for teenagers? Could you send information? Rice is my life!

But before I commit myself completely to a lifetime of working for Uncle Ben's, I have questions about your organization, and rice in general. First of all, who was/is Uncle Ben? You only show his *face* on your boxes. Was he the founder of your company? Was he related to Aunt Jemima? Was he tall? Fat? Devoted to family? I'm dying to know!

Secondly, I have a question about the connection between rice and weddings. How odd it is that we routinely pelt the married couple with handfuls of the stuff as they exit the church! How did this start? Why rice? Why not potato chips, or croutons, or M & M's? Did your company have anything to do with the custom? If so, that's pretty crafty! How much of Uncle Ben's annual profits can be attributed to "wedding sales?" Do you offer cheaper rice for weddings, since it'll wind up in the trash anyway? I'm intrigued!

Well, enough of my probing! I'm sure you guys/gals are busy making rice around the clock, and have little patience for reading lengthy letters. But if you could spare the time, I'd appreciate a response. I'm only seventeen, but my goal is to one day be the CEO of Uncle Ben's! Any literature that would point me in the right direction, as well as address my above questions, would be *greatly* appreciated! Thanks, and remember my name!

Rice is Nice,

Paul Rosa

Paul C. Rosa

P.S. Are there any Uncle Ben's T-shirts available? I'd be honored to wear one!!

Uncle Ben's, Inc.

5721 Harvey Wilson Drive
P. O. Box 1752
Houston, Texas 77251-1752 U.S.A.
Telephone 713-674-9484

Cable Address Bensrice
Telex 775380
Telex 377819
Fax 713-670-2227

19 October 1993

Mr. Paul C. Rosa
P.O. Box 9368
Colo. Springs, CO 80932

Dear Mr. Rosa:

We are in receipt of your letter of October 2, and, of course, we are sorry you did not receive our mailing to you on September 3, 1993.

A packet of information was sent to you, including: The Story of Uncle Ben; Facts About U.S. Rice, Story of UNCLE BEN'S® CONVERTED® Brand Rice, and How Rice Comes to Market. This material contains information about Uncle Ben's as well as rice in general. We are at a loss to understand why you did not receive the material as it was sent to the same address as was printed on your most recent correspondence.

Nevertheless, we are enclosing that information again for your review.

Concerning the summer intern program at Uncle Ben's, we do not have intern positions for high school students.

Secondly, we have no idea where the custom of throwing rice at weddings began. If you should research this subject, we would be interested in knowing as well.

We are sorry that an Uncle Ben's T-shirt is not available. We had some printed during our sponsorship of the 1992 Olympic Games, but our supply is now exhausted.

We trust all of your questions have now been answered, and the information will be helpful to you. Also, we would like to take this opportunity to send you some recipes and cents off coupons which can be used toward future purchases of Uncle Ben's products.

Thanks again for your interest in UNCLE BEN'S®.

Sincerely,

Nell Hopson
Consumer Affairs &
Administration Manager

P.O. Box 9368
Colo. Springs, CO 80932
August 30, 1993

Consumer Affairs
Super Glue Corporation
Hollis, NY 11423

Dear Adhesive Advisors,

I'll get straight to the point!! I am sitting in front of my typewriter with one hand hopelessly adhered to a portion of a large ceramic vase. With my lone "available" hand, I desperately transcribe my cry for help.

Nine days ago I purchased the aforementioned vase for my mother's 60th birthday, which falls on September 20. She has an extensive vase collection (over 800), and I found one that would surely have made her proud to call me "son," instead of "unemployed loser." When I returned from Sears with my purchase, I descended the stairs of my basement apartment, and tripped over my sleeping cat (Agnes). With a shriek, I tumbled downward, sending the vase soaring against the wall, where it promptly broke into three pieces. After I finished scolding Agnes ("Bad Agnes!" I screamed at her, as she knows she shouldn't nap on the stairs), I sadly picked up the remains of the devalued birthday present, and considered my options. This is when the *real* trouble began!

Since I had some Super Glue in my closet, I decided to try repairing the vase. I realized my mother has terrible eyesight, and surely wouldn't notice the imperfections. Anyway, clumsy oaf that I am, I spilled a large portion of glue on my left hand, and became hopelessly bonded to a sixteen inch (two pounds!) chunk of porcelain. No matter how hard I tugged, the offending material could not be removed. Soon I realized that I had quite the dilemma! Since I am a terribly shy person (almost reclusive) I couldn't just go to a doctor and receive treatment, and I am far too embarrassed to ask my few friends (Irene, Rafael, and Dave) for help.

So for the past nine days I have despaired in my apartment, unable to come up with a solution to my bizarre predicament. I was going to *call* your company, but my phone was recently stolen by some hoodlums, along with my Scott Turow novels. That is why I am writing you this urgent letter. What should I do?! How can I get this cursed vase fragment off of my hand without leaving the house?! The situation has graduated from an amusing blunder to a maddening nightmare. I am pleading with you to write to me **immediately** with some advice! I am running out of food! Thank you and god bless!

In Hell,

Paul Rosa

Paul C. Rosa

On September 17, 1993 I was delighted to receive a Federal Express package from the Super Glue Corporation, containing a loaf of Home Pride Hearty, Multi-Grain Bread (net wt. 24 Oz.) and a bottle of Super Glue Remover (net 0.5 Fl. Oz.). I felt better instantly!

Super Glue

CORPORATION   184-08 Jamaica Ave., Hollis, NY 11423 USA • 718 454-4747 • Fax 718 454-2947 • 1 800 221-4478

P.O. Box 9368
Colo. Springs, CO 80932
December 21, 1993

Mr. Nick Grooters
Super Glue (Pacer Technology)
9420 Santa Anita Ave.
Rancho Cucamonga, CA 91730

Dear Mr. Grooters ("Nick" from now on),

Super Glue is the sort of compassionate corporation that one usually only dares dream about!
When I wrote to you on August 30, 1993, I was truly a despondent man. As you recall, I had
glued a large chunk of vase to my left hand and was growing absolutely desperate. I explained
that the porcelain simply could not be removed, but I was too shy to visit a doctor or even leave
the house! Trapped in my apartment with little food (and less hope), I drafted a letter to you
which was, quite simply, a cry for help! Damn it, I had nowhere else to turn, Nick!

Well, shortly thereafter, when my last remaining morsel of food had already been ingested,
I received a (Federal Express!) package "from the gods!" Okay, it wasn't really from the gods, it
was (you guessed it, Nick) from *you*, my friend! Enclosed was a tasty loaf of Home Pride Hearty,
Multi-Grain Bread and (more importantly) a bottle of Super Glue Remover! Let me tell you, I
released a shriek of joy that sent my cat (Agnes) bolting for cover. Within moments I was free of
the "cursed porcelain" (my little nickname for the offending matter), and munching happily on a
nutritious slice of bread. My hope was instantly restored, Nick! My company (United Espresso
Coffee-Makers) allowed me to return to work (after considerable explaining), and my world was
soon returned to normal! I even began dating a lovely typewriter repairwoman (Rachel) and
exercising on the Stairmaster at the YMCA!

Nick, maybe I knew my luck couldn't last, but *you* may have a hard time believing what happened
last week. While repairing a broken Nigerian statuette with a bottle of Super Glue, I suddenly
sneezed, spilling a substantial quantity of glue on the lid of the nearby bottle of Super Glue
Remover you sent. Not only did I seal shut the opening of the Super Glue Remover, Nick, but as
I clumsily attempted to clean up the spill with a small chamois, I moronically adhered the bottle to
my right hand! "This can ***not*** be happening to me!" I bellowed to the heavens, once again
sending Agnes under the bed.

Well it's nightmare number two, Nick, but I knew I could write to you for help! I was so
humiliated that I told Rachel I was leaving town "for awhile." I'm (again) running low on food
and ask you (for the final time, I promise!) to send *another* bottle of Super Glue Remover.
A candy bar (Kit-Kat or Snickers) would be a nice touch as well! Also, please let me know if
something similar has happened before, and send *all* available information on your benevolent
organization. A (XL) T-shirt would be welcome as well. God bless you!

More than a little embarrassed,

Paul Rosa

Paul C. Rosa

No
Further
Response !

P.O. Box 9368
Colo. Springs, CO 80932
September 2, 1993

Omaha Steaks International
4400 South 96th Street
Omaha, NE 68103

Hello, Meat Lovers!

For many years now I have enjoyed your delicious steaks, and feel that they make the earth a better place to live! My all time favorite meal is an Omaha Steak (covered with A-1 sauce), corn on the cob, buttered rolls, and Michelob Light beer. For dessert, give me a slice of Sara Lee cheese cake. Yahoo, that's living!! I plan to continue my association with your company until the day I die. Yep, I'm hooked!

Given that your organization relies heavily on *cows* for its success, I felt I should come to you with the questions I had about this noble beast. Your diligence in this matter is appreciated, as I know this is an unusual request. But since I figured you were experts on cows, it would be foolish to query elsewhere. So, without further ado, I would like to get information on the following:

- Although they are now obviously domesticated, did cows once run wild? If so, did they run in packs, or were they loners?
- Can you ride a cow like a horse? I know they are considerably slower, but will they tolerate a saddle? How fast can they run at full gallop?
- When you see a field full of cows, is one of them the "leader?" Do the others look up to this cow for "guidance?"
- If you aggravate a cow a great deal, will they attack? If so, how do they inflict damage? Kick? Bite? Spit? Could a cow *kill* a guy?
- Why do they usually all face the same way when they graze? Wouldn't that make it easier for predators to sneak up on them?
- If you drive by some cows, and make "mooing" noises, do they enjoy that, or does it anger them?
- Cows seem to eat constantly! Do they have any "hobbies" or "games" to break up the monotony?
- They seem to like horses, but do cows like other animals? Cats? Sheep? Emus? Geese? Hamsters?

Although I have many other questions (cows clearly fascinate me), I don't want to take up too much of your valuable time. If you could respond with some detailed information, I would be eternally grateful! I look forward to your letter, my friends!

I'd like to "meat" you,

Paul Rosa

Paul C. Rosa

P.O. Box 9368
Colo. Springs, CO 80932
October 8, 1993

Consumer Affairs
Omaha Steaks International
4400 South 96th Street
Omaha, NE 68103

Dear flesh fanciers,

Well, it's been over five weeks since I wrote to Omaha Steaks International complimenting you on your meats. Perhaps I should have done some research into your customer service policies before being so generous with my praise. Five weeks is *plenty* of time to respond to a letter, even for a busy organization like yours! As a veteran of the Panamanian conflict, I assumed that I could be treated with respect in this country! But it also occurred to me that my correspondence may have been misplaced or mutilated by the (usually reliable) postal service. For this reason, I am re-submitting my original letter (September 2, 1993) for your perusal. I hope this time I will not be disappointed, my friends.

My first letter asked many questions, but since I mailed it, I've come up with several more. As I now presumably have your undivided attention, I'm posing them here:

① Which state consumes the most steak per capita? Oregon?
② Which parts of the cow aren't edible (other than bone)?
③ How long "could" a cow live?
④ Do vegetarians sometimes picket your facility?
⑤ Do you offer (XL) T-shirts?

I would be grateful if you could quickly address these questions as well as those in my first letter (thirteen total). I have a birthday coming up (11/17), and I'd like to order a large supply of meat. But I simply can not tolerate rude behavior. Thank you for your time and God bless.

Well done,

Paul Rosa

Paul C. Rosa

P.S. If a reply *has* been sent, please accept my apologies.

Omaha Steaks ®
International ®

CORPORATE MARKETING OFFICE

10909 JOHN GALT BOULEVARD
P.O. BOX 3300 • OMAHA, NEBRASKA 68103
PHONE (402) 597-3000 • TOLL FREE 1-800-228-2778
FAX NO. (402) 597-8222

October 12, 1993

Mr. Paul C. Rosa
P.O. Box 9368
Colo. Springs, CO 80932

Dear Mr. Rosa:

Your letters of September 2nd and October 8th were referred
to me today. My apologies to you because we did not respond
to your first letter in a more timely way.

I do not have answers to many of your questions. However, I
am enclosing brochures from the National Cattlemen's
Association and the Nebraska Beef Council that may provide
you with some answers.

One brochure concerns beef production and the other answers
questions about beef consumption. The third has answers
concerning how inedible cattle products are used to benefit
people.

With regard to the questions in your most recent letter:

1.   There are no industry figures on which state consumes
the most steak. The American Meat Institute publishes meat
consumption records by year and country but provides no
information on state-by-state consumption.

2.   Regarding what parts of cattle are not edible, please
see the enclosed brochure "Compliments of Cattle."

3.   I have no information on how long a cow could live.

4.   We have never been picketed by any vegetarian
organization.

5.   We regret that we do not have T-shirts available.

The National Cattlemen's Association is located in Denver.
They might be able to answer your earlier questions or refer
you to some reference materials. Their phone number in
Englewood, CO is 303-694-0305.

I hope these materials will answer at least a few of your
questions.

Our very best wishes to you for a happy birthday and for a
good and healthful year ahead.

Sincerely,

Marilyn Pred

Marilyn Pred, APR
Director of Public Relations

MP/ms
Enclosures

Paul Paul Rosa Rosa
P.O. P.O. Box Box 9368 9368
Colo. Colo. Springs Springs,, Co Co 80932 80932
September September 4 4,, 1993 1993

Personnel Personnel Office Office
Xerox Xerox Corporation Corporation
P.O. P.O. Box Box 1600 1600
Stamford Stamford,, CT CT 06904 06904

Dear Dear Xerox Xerox,,

Since Since a a boating boating accident accident in in 1984 1984,, I I have have been been cursed cursed with with the the affliction affliction you you are are already already probably probably aware aware of of.. I I apparently apparently damaged damaged the the part part of of the the brain brain that that prevents prevents repetitive repetitive behavior behavior.. What What psychiatrists psychiatrists would would ordinarily ordinarily label label as as obsessive-compulsive obsessive-compulsive behavior behavior,, is is in in my my case case simply simply an an untreatable untreatable injury injury.. This This is is the the way way I I talk talk,, the the way way I I write write,, and and even even the the way way I I type type!! It's It's often often an an embarrassing embarrassing nuisance nuisance,, but but I've I've learned learned to to live live with with it it..

Sadly Sadly enough enough,, there's there's a a lot lot of of prejudice prejudice out out there there,, and and I'm I'm having having a a real real tough tough time time finding finding a a job job!! Although Although I I graduated graduated from from college college ((after after eight eight years years,, ironically ironically enough enough)) last last spring spring with with a a 4.0 4.0 grade grade point point average average,, I I can't can't ever ever seem seem to to get get past past the the first first job job interview interview!! They They all all say say I I have have to to correct correct my my "condition" "condition" before before they they can can consider consider hiring hiring me me.. I I think think that's that's discrimination discrimination,, don't don't you you??

Then Then it it hit hit me me:: I I should should contact contact Xerox Xerox!! Since Since you you are are in in the the business business of of *duplication duplication,,* it it would would be be the the <u>perfect perfect</u> place place for for me me,, who who duplicates duplicates everything everything as as well well!! I've I've heard heard you you are are an an equal equal opportunity opportunity employer employer,, so so I I decided decided to to write write to to you you!! Would Would you you be be willing willing to to interview interview me me?? I I think think you'd you'd be be impressed impressed,, my my friends friends!! Please Please *write write* to to me me with with your your thoughts thoughts -- I I don't don't use use phones phones ((you you can can understand understand)).. Thank Thank you you so so much much,, and and god god bless bless!!

Redundantly Redundantly yours yours,,

Paul Paul C. C. Rosa Rosa

Paul Paul C. C. Rosa Rosa

P.S. P.S. Do Do you you have have any any ((XL XL)) T-shirts T-shirts??

Paul Paul Rosa Rosa
P.O. P.O. Box Box 9368 9368
Colo. Colo. Springs Springs,, Co Co 80932 80932

Personnel Personnel Office Office
Xerox Xerox Corporation Corporation
P.O. P.O. Box Box 1600 1600
Stamford Stamford ,, CT CT 06904 06904

October 21, 1993

Mr. Paul Rosa
P.O. Box 9368
Colo. Springs, CO 80932

Dear Mr. Rosa:

Thank you for your recent correspondence expressing interest in pursuing employment opportunities with Xerox Corporation.

We have had an opportunity to explore possible opportunities based on your background and interest. Unfortunately, we have no positions available where we could fully utilize your career objectives and experience.

We wish you success in satisfying your career plans and thank you for considering Xerox as a prospective employer.

Per your request, enclosed is and XL T-Shirt.

Sincerely,

Patricia A. Pia

Patricia A. Pia
Manager,
Human Resources Operations

PAP/efl

T-Shirt
Received!

P.O. Box 9368
Colo. Springs, CO 80932
September 5, 1993

Hallmark Cards (Employment Office)
2501 McGee Rd.
Kansas City, MO 64108

Dear Wordsmiths,

I have been a tremendous fan of your company for many years! For almost every special occasion, I make my way to the local book store and purchase the perfect card for my loved one or acquaintance. It is with tremendous confidence that I mail (or hand) the card to "that special person." The rest of the day is spent in a pleasant "haze," knowing that I've brightened the day of someone who is important to me. Your entire organization (from the mailboy to the CEO) is to be congratulated!!

Since I was a sophomore in college (Grinnell College in Iowa), I have fantasized about the possibility of working for Hallmark. But my father (damn him!) *insisted* that I pursue a career as a Food Service Manager, and continue the family tradition - four generations - of working in a Ramada Inn Restaurant. So, I foolishly listened to the bastard, instead of my heart, and the last sixteen years have been passed with a feeling of uneasiness, knowing I have selected the wrong career path. Oh, don't get me wrong, I've done alright for myself. I married a magnificent woman (Judi), and we are raising nine wonderful children, one of whom (Ben) has been tested at a 137 IQ level! He'll never work at a Ramada; My father died in a boating accident, so the pressure's off!

Anyway, I've been thinking about my lifelong dream of working for Hallmark as a *poetry submitter*. Judi keeps telling me to present some of the work I've compiled over the years, and I'm finally doing it!! Here are some of the best poems I've written since 1977, and I offer them for your (critical!) review:

When I think of you, I think of love.
Our personalities fit just like a glove!
You smell as sweet as summer dew.
If someone hurts you, that day he'll rue!
(Anniversary) ©1977, Paul Rosa

It's your birthday, my pet, you're twenty-three!
You flit about like a bumble bee.
When you "buzz" around my kitchen door,
I assure you, my sweet, it's you I adore!
(Birthday) ©1984, Paul Rosa

Mom, you're great, like Mahatma Gandhi!
You raised me right, and it was all for free.
But now I'm older, and have some money.
Just lettin' you know, you're still my honey!
(Mother's Day) ©1990, Paul Rosa

You type my reports with nary a grumble.
You look nice, and boy are you humble!
Your computer skills are the envy of all,
But today is your day, so go to the mall!
(Secretary's Day) ©1993, Paul Rosa

Well, what do you think?! Do you think there's some potential there? I would sure appreciate it if you could write to me and let me know the employment opportunities (I can relocate)! Thank you so much, and keep making America happy! Also, if you have any (XL) T-shirts, I'd love to have one!

Rhyming is fun,

Paul Rosa

Paul C. Rosa

Hallmark Cards

September 28, 1993

Mr. Paul Rosa
P.O. Box 9368
Colo. Springs, CO 80932

Dear Paul:

Thank you for your recent inquiry and for the interest you have expressed in exploring job possibilities at Hallmark. Our writers are versatile idea people who provide original copy in a wide variety of styles for all of our products. Some focus their talents on traditional forms of prose and verse. Others work exclusively on writing humor. And still others are able to do both.

Hallmark editors work closely with line designers to assure the right blending of words and artwork for maximum appeal. Some concentrate on greeting cards and some on non-card products such as posters, party goods, calendars, stickers, puzzles, plaques and mugs. They also work with the writers to develop fresh, innovative copy for each product line. This requires excellent language skills and the ability to work effectively with creative teams.

Since we require such a specialized kind of editing and writing, we ask all applicants interested in full-time employment to complete the enclosed Writer/Editor Portfolio. After you have submitted your completed application form and Portfolio, a panel of Writing and Editorial managers will review your work. You will be notified of the results of the review within a few weeks. If you'd like to retain a copy of the portfolio for your records, please do so now--as the original cannot be returned to you. We hope, also, that you understand that we cannot critique your Portfolio.

Again, thank you for your interest in Hallmark..

Sincerely,

James Marsh

James Marsh
Administrative Assistant
Creative Staffing and Development

Enclosure: Writer/Editor Portfolio

P.O. Box 9368
Colo. Springs, CO 80932
September 6, 1993

Consumer Affairs
U.S. West Direct White and Yellow Pages
198 Inverness Drive West
P.O. Box 6572
Englewood, CO 80155-6572

Dear Phone Friends,

I have used your telephone book ("The White & Yellow Pages") for over twenty-five years, and have been consistently impressed with it's accuracy and ease of use! It is a pleasure to deal with a product that does exactly what it's supposed to do! "Keep up the terrific work!" is the sentiment I extend to you fine folks!

But last Tuesday something occurred in my family (including thirteen children: Toni, Pernis, Rufon, Lee Isna, Renii, Anwar, Kiki, Timmi, Shakla, Sylvis, Bantar, Jacki, and Ed). We all decided (Ed was the exception) that the name "The **White** and **Yellow** Pages" is <u>racist</u>! You see, I am an African-American and my wife, Tunna, is an American Indian (Apache). After a three hour family discussion at the dinner table, we concluded that this name "favors" Caucasians and Orientals, as it features their *skin colors*!

Why must the pages be white and yellow every year?! Why not "black" and "red" occasionally (we'd be flattered), or any of the other fabulous skin tones featured worldwide? The combinations are vast and exciting, and should be taken advantage of! Pairing, say, white pages with light brown pages could teach people that Caucasians and Iranians can/should get along! "The Black & Yellow Pages" would teach us that African-Americans and Koreans can live in harmony!! You see, you could come out with dozens of varieties every year, each showing us how important it is to "stand side by side," just like the pages of your book! My family was so moved by the idea, that we invited dozens of (ethnically diverse) neighbors to our house the following day to enjoy spaghetti and a stirring video-tape (Dead Poets' Society). It was a terrific, loving evening, and most of the attendees agreed with our phone book suggestion!!

So, what do you think of my idea of ***"cultural healing through phone book diversity?"*** Wouldn't you be proud to distribute such colorful, educational publications? If you could spare the time, my family would certainly be impressed with a swift reply! My youngest daughter, Jacki, is now working on a school project dealing with the very subject outlined in this letter. For her sake, if not for our society as a whole, please write soon, my friends!

Alphabetically yours,

Paul Rosa

Paul C. and Tunna Rosa

P.S. Please send a (XL) T-shirt for my oldest boy, Toni, age 17.

Facsimile 303 784-1478

Cal Pierce
Market Development Analyst

September 21, 1993

Paul Rosa & Family
P.O. Box 9368
Colo. Springs, CO 80932

Dear Mr. Rosa:

Thank you for contacting U S WEST Direct regarding the Colorado Springs directory. U S WEST Direct is a customer focused organization therefore we are sensitive and responsive to your needs and concerns.

Your commendations to us for "producing a product that does what it's supposed to do" is greatly appreciated. It's always nice to hear that our product is meeting the customer's needs. Your letter also suggested that because our directory is called the "White and Yellow Pages," racial intent is implied. Being a customer focused organization does not afford us the leisure of disagreeing with our customers, but in rare instances, exceptions are sometimes made.

Besides constituting a marketing strategy that differentiates our products on the marketplace, our directories are white and yellow because of tradition. You see...U S WEST Direct is a company that is richly embedded in tradition. A tradition of serving our customers. A tradition of community obligation. A tradition of respect for people. All people. We pride ourselves on having a diverse employment body that mirrors the communities in which we serve.

You closed your letter by mentioning that your daughter, Jacki, is working on a school project dealing with the subject outlined in this letter and that our response will affect her report. I would like to close by asking Jacki to look inside the Colorado Springs book. She will find the colors white, black, green, yellow, red, and blue. This may emphasize the danger in "judging a book by its' cover" or in this case "an organization by its' book." Good day, Mr. Rosa.

Sincerely,

T-shirt Received !

Cal Pierce
Market Development Analyst

I have enclosed a complimentary T-shirt as you have requested. You stated that your son Ed disagreed with the family's position on our directory. This T-shirt is not for Toni but for Ed. Not only was Ed correct, he also exemplified outstanding courage and conviction in his beliefs. My compliments, Ed. Enjoy.

Ed Rosa
c/o Ms. Nicole Rosa
160 Glenfield Dr.
Colo. Springs, CO 80968

Mr. Cal Pierce
Market Development Analyst
U S West Direct
198 Inverness Drive West
Englewood, CO 80112

Dear Mr. Pierce,

Thank you so much for the cool Yellow Pages T-shirt. I wore it to school last week (I'm in the tenth grade with a 4.0 grade point average), and all the other kids asked where I got it! I know my father asked for a shirt for Toni, and I thought it was very nice that you sent it to me instead. But Toni is a really good guy, so could you send *me* another one (XL) so I can surprise him. That would be terrific, sir!

I read your letter to my father, and agreed with you completely. To say that your company is racist because of the colors of the phone book pages is <u>really</u> <u>stupid</u> I think! I liked it when you said "there was a danger in judging a book by its cover or an organization by its book." That was really clever and it put my father in his place. He's kind of a bully, and people usually back down from him because he's 6'9". Good work!

Yes, my father is a bit strange. He's *always* writing dumb letters, accusing companies of a number of things. He wrote to Motel 6, complaining that the rooms were "too plain." It's a budget hotel, for God's sake! He wrote to Domino's Pizza, asking if the pizza had to arrive (in 30 minutes) at the front door or in the driveway on time. That's craziness! And he accused *Ivory* soap of using rhinoceros horns in their product (get real, dad!). Living with him is very annoying, as I almost always disagree with his ideas. My twelve brothers and sisters always "kiss up" to him, but I refuse to do the same. This can be tough, though.

I liked it when you said I "exemplified outstanding courage and conviction!" Dad never says those things to me, and it makes me sad. Can you give me some advice on sticking to one's beliefs through thick and thin? I'd appreciate any pointers you can offer since you seem to be a successful man. I'm planning to go to Yale and would certainly like to hear some tips!

As my father sometimes reads my mail, could you please send a letter to my aunt's (above) address? She'll give it to me without showing him. Thanks, Mr. Pierce, and don't forget that T-shirt for Toni. His birthday is October 20.

Sincerely,

Ed Rosa

Ed Rosa

U S WEST Direct
A Division of
U S WEST Marketing Resources Group, Inc.
198 Inverness Drive West
Englewood, Colorado 80112
303 784-1132

Facsimile 303 784-1478

Cal Pierce
Market Development Analyst

USWEST
DIRECT Ⓐ

September 30, 1993

Mr. Ed Rosa
c/o Ms. Nicole Rosa
160 Glenfield Dr.
Colo. Springs, CO 80968

Dear Ed:

After reading your letter, I was thoroughly impressed with your maturity and sophistication at such a young age. You expressed yourself well. I must admit that when I was in the tenth grade, I could not compose such a letter. I was too pre-occupied with sports.

You asked that I give you advice on "sticking to one's beliefs through thick and thin." Ed, I feel that you have this *conviction* thing mastered. You have demonstrated this by maintaining a perfect grade point average and choosing a fine institution (Yale) to further your education. Knowing that there are youths such as yourself in the community reconfirms my confidence in the next generation. The only advice I can give to you is "keep up the great work!" Your parents must be very proud.

Enclosed you will find the T-shirt you requested for your brother Toni. It was a pleasure hearing from you and I wish you well in all your endeavors.

Sincerely,

Cal Pierce
Market Development Analyst

T-shirt Received!!

P.O. Box 9368
Colo. Springs, CO 80932
September 8, 1993

Consumer Affairs
Hershey Foods Corp.
100 Mansion Road East
Hershey, PA 17033

Dear Sugar Daddies,

Yes, I love chocolate. But I *really* love Hershey Bars! They are smooth, delicious and absolute heaven to eat! When I was a small lad, growing up in Twisp, Washington (pop.872), my mother limited my candy bar intake to five a week. I always thought this was ridiculous because chocolate is wonderful and shouldn't be rationed. But I was too young to effectively fight her on this, and the rule remained intact. I just counted the days until I could leave home and determine my own eating habits!

In 1985 I enrolled at Flagler College in Florida, far from my mother's stifling rules and regulations! As I prepared myself for my current career as an ichthyologist (fish scientist), I also indulged myself completely in my beloved chocolate. Soon I was eating seven to ten Hershey Bars a day, and, on occasion, as many as fifteen. Mental health experts would probably suggest that I was trying to "get even" with my mother, but they would be missing the point completely! Damn it, I love chocolate, that's all! As I finished my college career - with a 3.61 grade point average - I was consuming as many as fifteen Hershey Bars a day, and feeling excited about the endless possibilities ahead! Granted, I now carried about 375 pounds on my 5'8" frame, but I'm not vain (Carly Simon wasn't singing about me!).

Anyway, in 1990 my girlfriend (Renii) and I settled in Colorado Springs. I secured a terrific position at a local aquarium, and Renii soon was hired as an administrator for a company which manufactures catnip toys for cats. We are young, happy, and very much in love. She shares my passion for chocolate, regularly consuming as many as ten bars per day! When my Hershey Bar Daily Consumption Average ("H.B.D.C.A." as we like to say!) reached about twenty last month, a strange and wonderful idea occurred to me.

Why not subsist on a diet consisting of nothing but Hershey Bars and, of course, beverages? I figure 200 bars a week would keep me well nourished *and* reduce my grocery bills by as much as 60%! Renii thinks it's a great idea too, but thought I should contact you first. So, what do you think? Is it sensible to live on nothing but chocolate? If so, can I buy huge quantities from you at a discount? Also, as I have consumed approximately **55,000** Hershey Bars in my life, I was curious if I've set some sort of record? Finally, are you hiring any chocolate consultants? I eagerly look forward to your reply, my friends!

Mothers don't *always* know best,

Paul Rosa

Paul C. (Charles, not chocolate) Rosa

P.S. Could you please send two (XL) T-shirts?

Hershey Chocolate U.S.A. P.O. Box 815, Hershey, PA 17033-0815 Phone: 1-800-468-1714

A Division of
Hershey Foods

September 27, 1993

Mr. Paul C. Rosa
P.O. Box 9368
Colo. Springs, CO 80932

Dear Mr. Rosa:

We appreciate your taking the time to let us know how much you enjoy our products.

We are proud of our commitment to excellence in manufacturing quality products. We are always pleased to hear from consumers who appreciate our efforts. Hershey has built its reputation on this tradition and we will continue to manufacture the superior quality products you enjoy.

Hershey Foods Corporation has provided consumers with information on its products in an open and forthright manner for many years. We are continuing our efforts to inform consumers about the health effects of fat and individual fatty acids, as well as the ingredient and nutrient content of our products. We were the first confectioner to place nutrition information on our product labels; and we continue to believe objective nutrition information on the food label is an appropriate and technically sound approach to nutrition education.

Standards of Identity set forth by the Food and Drug Administration (FDA), establish a rigid set of identifications which designate for each chocolate and cocoa product the percentage of key ingredients that must be present in order for them to bear the name of such product. Milk chocolate must contain no less than 3.66% milk fat (butterfat), no less than 12% milk solids, and at least 10% chocolate liquor.

Hershey believes that a healthy diet includes room for snack foods like chocolate that taste good and provide nutritional value. Chocolate is one food that deserves attention for its individual merit. Chocolate products make a positive contribution to a well-balanced diet since they are composed of many wholesome ingredients such as whole milk, almonds, peanuts, granola, sugar and chocolate. Many in the scientific community believe that individual food items should not be singled out—it is the overall diet that is important. Any food that contributes to the required daily caloric level provides benefit.

Page 2

Thank you for your interest in our company.

Sincerely,

Fran Long
Consumer Respondent

P.O. Box 9368
Colo. Springs, CO 80932
September 8, 1993

Mayor of Colorado Springs
Robert Isaac
P.O. Box 1575
Colorado Springs, CO 80901

Dear Mayor Isaac (may I call you Bob?),

For a long time I've been a big fan of yours, and thought it was high time I let you know. I consistently vote for you because I agree with most of your decisions. You are a breath of fresh air in today's "polluted" world of overblown do-nothings! Keep it up, my friend! As I know you are open to suggestions from concerned citizens, I thought it would be wise to contact you!

This may sound a bit weird at first, but I think, in time, you'll find my idea terrific. When Colorado Springs suffered through some nasty, rainy days recently, something occurred to me: Why not put the entire city under a gigantic, transparent dome? It's never been done on a scale larger than athletic stadiums, but it is certainly architecturally feasible (I asked my brother, Tony, who is a landscaper). When the weather is nice and sunny, the roof can be retracted to drench the populace in sunshine. When it rains, the roof would be closed to *keep* the people from getting drenched! Also, during the winter, the dome can be closed *and* heated to keep the citizens toasty and warm. Conversely, the stifling summer months could be cooled with the world's largest air-conditioner! Naturally, there would be holes "punched" in the side of the dome to allow cars and pedestrians free passage.

Sure, the project would cost a few hundred thousand dollars, but think of the added tourism! Folks from all over North America (and Japan) would joyfully flock to see **"The Dome!"** Out-of-towners could pay a $5.00 toll as they enter the city, and the whole project would pay for itself in a few years! We would be the envy of all who visited! Soon, people would begin moving here because of the benefits of the dome, and before you know it, we'd be one of the biggest cities in America!

So, what do you think, Bob? Do you like my idea? Aren't you surprised that it didn't occur to *you*? If this project does get off the ground (get it?), will I receive some sort of compensation? That would be great, because I'm tired of my job as a dog groomer. Please let me know your opinions on my plan (a letter from you would certainly be cherished!).

Democratically yours,

Paul Rosa

Paul C. Rosa

P.S. Do you have any (XL) T-shirts?

ROBERT M. ISAAC
MAYOR

CITY OF COLORADO SPRINGS

September 15, 1993

Paul C. Rosa
P.O. Box 9368
Colo. Springs, CO 80932

Dear Mr. Rosa:

Thank you for your letter of September 8 and your kind comments. As for your suggestion, I have referred it to the City Administration for comment.

Sincerely,

Robert M. Isaac
Mayor

c: City Manager

P.O. Box 9368
Colo. Springs, CO 80932
September 14, 1993

Promotions Department
Ultra Snuggle Fabric Softener
Lever Brothers Company
New York, NY 10022

Dear Laundry Lads and Ladies,

Your fabric softener makes my monthly visit to the Laundromat (or is it "Laundrymat?") a true pleasure. Ultra Snuggle leaves my clothes feeling "pillowy" soft and smelling like Vermont in autumn. I grew up in Brattleboro, VT (pop. 8,596), so I should know, my fragrant friends! My family of seventeen may be your biggest customer - we all use Ultra Snuggle!

But in July 22 of this year I was watching one of your television commercials featuring the **"Snuggle Bear"** character, and something occurred to me: I <u>hate</u> that cute little bastard!! Not only do I hate him, I want him "dead!" I realize he is only a fictitious character, but my disdain for him is so complete, that I felt it was my responsibility to write.

But first I conducted a survey of complete strangers while I traveled the country this summer (I sell quality aquarium accessories). After asking 1,275 people what they thought of your "mascot", 72% said they disliked or hated the little creature, 15% said they were indifferent, 9% said they liked or loved him, and 4% asked me to leave them alone. With my report in hand -I can send it if you wish- I am now urging you to *destroy* Snuggle Bear in one of your commercials! I predict your sales would then skyrocket, since so many folks despise him! And now, without further ado, I offer suggestions for Snuggle Bear's television demise:

1. Snuggle Bear gets tossed into a clothes dryer and is baked to death.
2. Snuggle Bear has a huge pile of dryer lint stuffed down his throat, asphyxiating him.
3. Snuggle Bear is crushed under a tremendous load of filthy laundry.
4. Snuggle Bear encounters a *real* bear and is torn asunder.
5. Snuggle Bear is forced to watch "Pat Sajak Show" reruns, dying of boredom.

I'd be happy to <u>give</u> you any of these ideas without reimbursement, but please, please kill him *somehow*. What do you think of my idea? Does it seem like a good one? I'm looking forward to your reply! I'd also like a (XL) T-shirt if you have one!

One hour martinized,

Paul Rosa

Paul C. Rosa

P.S. What do you think of Maytag's "Lonely Repairman" character?

Promotions Department
Ultra Snuggle Fabric Softener
Lever Brothers Company
New York, NY 10022

Dear Softies,

It has now been approximately six weeks since I sent a letter to Ultra Snuggle (September 14, 1993). As you recall, I complimented you on your superior fabric softener and explained that my entire family (fifteen children!) loves the stuff. I bet we use more of this product than any one family in North America! Do you keep any statistics? As a faithful customer (what an understatement!) of Ultra Snuggle, I assumed my letter would be given some sort of priority. Never did I imagine that my correspondence would go unanswered! Well, my friends, as a veteran of the Watts riots (LAPD), I feel I've certainly earned the right to an answer within six weeks. Don't you? I trust you answered, "yes."

Admittedly, my first letter wasn't entirely complimentary, as I pushed for the demise of Snuggle Bear. I even suggested some possibilities for his "death," and this might have upset you. Keep in mind, I would never encourage any type of cruelty toward animals (we have four cocker spaniels: Kiki, Tina, Rusty, and Vladimir). But I feel that animated characters are fair game. For this reason, I encouraged you to "do him in" by stuffing dryer lint down his throat, baking him in a dryer, etc. Remember, the "casual" poll I conducted revealed that 72% of America's citizens simply don't like the little creature. A funny commercial ending his "life" would be greeted with hoots of approval, I think. But, I assure you, no disrespect was intended!

In the spirit of fair play, I've decided to re-submit my first letter, with a polite request that you respond immediately. Raising fifteen children leaves little time for frivolous letter writing! If you found my ideas for Snuggle Bear's doom too...brutal, I'd be happy to come up with some gentler, more politically-correct ideas (i.e. Snuggle Bear dies while fighting terrorists). So please get back to me at once with your thoughts on my ideas, and keep up the exemplary work! Finally, please send a (XL) T-shirt for my oldest boy, Wip. God bless.

Fluffin' and Foldin',

Paul Rosa

Paul C. Rosa

LEVER

Mr. Paul C. Rosa
P.O. Box 9368
Colo. Springs, CO 80932

Dear Mr. Rosa:

Please accept our apology for the delay in responding to your letter of November 18, 1993. Your most recent communication of December 21st to our President, Charles Strauss, has been referred to me for reply.

Lever Brothers' Snuggle Bear has been a highly effective part of our advertising campaign for many years. As you can appreciate, such campaigns are based on extensive market research. At this time, we have no plans to change our product message. Also, since we rely upon the expertise of Lever Brothers personnel and specially selected agencies to design and execute our advertising campaigns, we do not accept unpatented ideas from individuals outside of our company.

Thank you for your interest in our company and its products.

Sincerely,

Kathryn S. Jones

Kathryn S. Jones
Manager Consumer Services

KSJ/ad

P.O. Box 9368
Colo. Springs, CO 80932
September 15, 1993

Records Review Committee
The Guinness Book of World Records
460 Park Avenue South
New York, NY 10016

Dear Record Keepers,

Since I was a small lad growing up in Millsboro, Delaware (pop. 1,233), I have excitedly welcomed the new Guinness Book of World Records each year. When it would arrive at our house I would disappear into the attic for several days, fascinated with the various records and achievements! My parents (Ed and Agnes) would bring my meals to me as I memorized page after page of information. I was very popular at school, as I knew the answers to all sorts of obscure questions. Hip, hip, hooray for the Guinness heroes!

I never dreamed that my name could appear in your book, but that all changed recently! On September 12, 1992 I decided to engage in an activity that would push me to my physical limit, as well as (hopefully) land me in your record book! I decided to pick up my cat, Jesse (she weighed only seven pounds), and carry her around for as long as I could. I began to haul her about for sixteen hours a day, releasing her only to sleep.

Yes, while I ate, shopped, showered and worked (I'm a used bookstore owner), Jesse was constantly in my arms! Granted, there were some trying times -holding Jesse over her litter box was a chore- but as a rule, we got along famously! My girlfriend (Cynthia) dumped me in January, but she could never understand my devotion to your publication, nor my driving desire to be a part of it. In time, Jesse became quite content with our arrangement, even jumping into my arms as I climbed out of bed each morning. Business at the bookstore boomed as news of my interesting endeavor spread. Unfortunately, Jesse, getting no exercise to speak of, ballooned to sixteen pounds. My biceps swelled to 22 inches, adjusting to the tremendous task at hand. In April I met my new girlfriend (Grace), and the three of us could often be seen strolling about town, happy as can be. I promised to marry Grace when my "cat toting" ended, and our wedding is slated for next August!

Finally, three days ago, I gently set portly Jesse down for good. I had carried her with me every waking hour for one year, and my pride was profound! I'd now like to know if I've set the record for cat carrying. If this is indeed the case, I'd be the happiest man to ever walk the face of North America! Please write to me quickly and give me the news...good or bad!

Purrfectly frank,

Paul Rosa

Paul C. Rosa

P.S. Please send a (XL) T-shirt.

**Facts On File®**

Facts On File, Inc.
460 Park Avenue South
New York, NY 10016-7382
212 683 2244
Telex 238552 FACTS UR
Fax 212 213 4578
212 683 3633

October 29, 1993

Paul C. Rosa
P.O. Box 9368
Colo. Springs, CO 80932

Dear Mr. Rosa:

Thank you for your inquiry concerning your "record" proposal to be included in "The Guinness Book of Records." This is a most unsual story and I believe it is the first of its type that we have received. For this reason it is very difficult for me to be able to say whether or not you have established any kind of record. While I certainly do not underestimate your proposal, I do think this item is too specialized for a reference book as general as "The Guinness Book of Records." I'm afraid that unique occurrences, interesting peculiarities, or "firsts" are not necessarily records and therefore are rerely included in the book.

I am sorry that I cannqt be more positive at this stage, however all letters are kept on file for possible future references. Thank you again for your inquiry and interest in "The Guinness Book of Records."

Sincerely yours,

Denise G. Jack
Editorial Assistant
U.S. edition

:dgj

P.O. Box 9368
Colo. Springs, CO 80932
September 16, 1993

Consumer Affairs
Seven-Eleven Corporation
P.O. Box 0711
Dallas, TX 75221

Dear Convenience Clique,

I'm a big man with a big thirst. Well, maybe that's an understatement. I'm an enormous man (6'9", 625 pounds), and I routinely consume 200-300 ounces of fluid a day! As a salesman of quality scarves and Windbreakers, I travel extensively throughout the midwest. I find that being on the road greatly contributes to my already powerful thirst (also, I drive an AMC Matador with no air-conditioner). I often stop at Seven-Eleven stores four or five times per day to purchase your superb snacks and refreshing carbonated beverages. Your colorful road signs serve as delightful beacons (if you will) on the horizon. Frankly, I don't know what I'd do without your terrific stores. As a strict Presbyterian, I say, "God bless you!"

And as a concerned customer, I'd like to share some ideas. You carry four sizes of drinks: Small = 16 oz., Big Gulp = 32 oz., Super Big Gulp = 44 0z., and Double Gulp = 64 oz. That's fine for most folks, but some of us have truly robust thirsts and need more! I generally buy a Double Gulp *plus* a Super Big Gulp (108 ounces total) to "extinguish the flame." But I must say that it is quite inconvenient to have two containers of liquid, especially while driving! For this reason, I recommend that you introduce a container which holds 128 ounces (just to be safe), and call it the Double Double Gulp. One gallon of refereshment should quell even the most monstrous thirst!

Also, as the enclosed materials illustrate, I will soon be engaging in another form of tremendous consumption. I will try to eat three 72 ounce steaks -in one hour- at the Big Texan Restaurant in Amarillo, Texas. No one has *ever* eaten 13.5 pounds of meat in one sitting, so, needless to say, I will need something to wash the huge pile of flesh down with! And then it occurred to me: How about some gigantic Seven-Eleven drinks? The association would be perfect (huge steaks with huge beverages!). If this record-breaking event is of interest to you, let me know! Sponsors are lining up now!

Finally, what does "Seven-Eleven" mean? My Mom joked that this was how many English words (between seven and eleven) your typical employees know. Stupidity like that simply doesn't warrant a response. I look forward to your reply, folks! And could you send a (XL) T-shirt?

Chili dogs are inviting,

Paul Rosa

Paul C. Rosa

November 2, 1993

Mr. Paul Rosa
P.O. Box 9368
Colo. Springs, CO 80932

Dear Mr. Rosa:

Thank you for writing us about your ideas for a Double Double Gulp and letting us know about the challenge in Amarillo. We enjoyed your letter and apologize for the delay in our response.

7-Eleven's commitment to its customers is to provide a broad selection of high-quality products and services that can be purchased with speed, at a fair price and in a clean, safe and friendly store environment. In an effort to meet this goal, we have passed along your idea to offer a larger fountain drink size to the appropriate category manager for consideration.

With respect to your request for 7-Eleven sponsorship, we recently reviewed our corporate giving and sponsorship program to see how we can better meet the diverse needs of the communities we serve. As a result, we have had to rethink our strategy and limit our available resources to two major areas -- literacy and programs that increase multi-cultural understanding -- in locations where we do business.

While your idea for 7-Eleven to provide a "gigantic" 7-Eleven fountain soft drink to go along with the three 72-oz. steaks is a novel one, unfortunately, it is not in line with our corporate giving strategy. Also, The Southland Corporation does not operate stores in Amarillo, so we would not be sponsoring an event there. However, we wish you much success at the Big Texan Restaurant.

To answer your final question, the name 7-Eleven was coined in 1946 for the hours the stores were open -- 7 a.m. to 11 p.m. In 1971, 7-Eleven began offering 24-hour convenience store service in many areas, and today almost all 7-Eleven stores are open round-the-clock.

We greatly value customer feedback such as yours, and to show our appreciation, we have enclosed a company history brochure and two coupons for a <u>free</u> 44 oz. Super Big Gulp. (Sorry, we currently don't have any 7-Eleven T-shirts.) The coupons can be redeemed at most participating 7-Eleven stores in Colorado Springs.

Sincerely,

Janey Camacho-King
Customer Relations Manager
7-Eleven Stores
2711 North Haskell Avenue / Dallas, Texas 75204-2906 / Phone (214) 828-7345

DIVISION OF
THE SOUTHLAND
CORPORATION

P.O. Box 9368
Colo. Springs, CO 80932
September 17, 1993

Customer Service
SPAM c/o Hormel Meats
500 NE 14th Ave.
Austin, MN 55912

Dear lunch meat lords,

What can I say? SPAM is the greatest food since popcorn! I eat the stuff constantly (15-20 times a week), but simply can't get enough of that delicious, juicy meat! Please tell the inventor of SPAM that he/she has made one young man in Colorado very happy, and, if at all possible, I'd love to get an informative letter! The history of SPAM has always intrigued me, but I've never known where to turn for answers...until now!!

I've been eating SPAM since 1979, my high school sophomore year in Jasper, AR (pop. 519). My girlfriend (and now, my wife), Becky Lee Holtzman offered me a bite of her SPAM sandwich in the cafeteria one day, and I almost screamed with pleasure! I still remember with great fondness our Saturday nights at the Mile High Drive-In, where we would watch scary movies and share the splendid SPAM and pickle submarine sandwiches she would lovingly create. Your company is truly a vital slice (no pun intended) of Americana . Go on, give your office-mate a congratulatory hug! Yes, do it now!

In 1984, now living in Wilton, Maine (pop. 2,225), I decided to test my devotion to SPAM. "How does a man test his devotion to SPAM?" you may be asking yourself or your (freshly-hugged) office-mate. Well, I'll tell you. Every spare dollar we had went toward purchasing cans of SPAM. Times were tough -I labored as an Orkin exterminator, wrestling with my personal objections to slaughtering *any* of God's creatures- and we could only afford 725 cans that year. But our luck changed (Becky Lee soon earned a good living as a welder), and by the beginning of 1986 we had over 2,200 cans. If you haven't guessed by now, we had decided to build our dream house entirely out of SPAM cans. Yes, it's true!

In 1988 we moved to Colorado Springs, and it required a U-Haul to transport our now impressive total of 8,100 cans. We prospered here, and the collection slowly grew to total 32,000 cans by March of this year. Our goal had been met, so my brother (Buck) and I began the difficult task of "cementing" can to can to can. But the work was a pleasure, and we passed the hours by bellowing old Bob Seger songs. The glorious three bedroom SPAM house has now been complete for two weeks, and Becky Lee and I couldn't be happier. And we have more friends than ever (SPAM is a real "people magnet").

So, thanks for the terrific product and the inspiration to "follow my heart." Every time I enter my driveway I am reminded of SPAM...an American icon! I'd be happy to send photographs or a video-tape if you are interested. And could you send a (XL) T-shirt? I look forward to your quick reply!

Housed in meat,

Paul Rosa

Paul C. Rosa

Consumer Affairs

Hormel Foods Corporation
1 Hormel Place
Austin MN 55912-3680

September 28, 1993

Mr Paul Rosa
P.O. Box 9368
Colo. Springs, CO 80932

Dear Mr Rosa,

Thank you for contacting us recently with your request for
SPAM related merchandise.

SPAM Luncheon Meat was first introduced in 1937 and has
enjoyed continuing success in the marketplace. We are
proud of the long history of SPAM Luncheon Meat and
particularly the role it played during World War II. The
military continues to be a faithful consumer of SPAM
Luncheon Meat and purchases millions of pounds of the
product every year.

The order information you requested is enclosed. Please
send your request and the appropriate dollar amount to the
address indicated.

Again, thank you for contacting us. We hope you enjoy the
items you order. We also hope you continue to enjoy SPAM
Luncheon Meat and other Hormel products available in your
area.

Sincerely,

Joan Davis

Joan Davis
Consumer Response Specialist
93674410

P.O. Box 9368
Colo. Springs, CO 80932
September 19, 1993

Consumer Affairs
Arm & Hammer Baking Soda Toothpaste
Church & Dwight Co., Inc.
Princeton, NJ 08540

Dear Tooth Titans,

I noticed that you are located in Princeton, N.J.! Ah, lovely Princeton, my boyhood home! Times were tough during the Depression, but my family (Mom, Pop, Becky Lee, Agnes, Zak, Terri, June, Ike, Ezekial, Karen, Penny, George, Kim, Chris, and myself) got along fine with the proper combination of love and fierce determination. Pop worked for a small insect exterminating company, constantly struggling with his belief that *all* animals should be treated with dignity and respect. He brought home barely sixty dollars a month, but we all managed to get enough to eat. It is with great nostalgia that I remember our evening strolls through the city (the university was so lovely!). Pop would challenge the kids to identify various plants, and Zak soon used his "education" by opening a flower shop in nearby Hopewell (pop. 2,001).

World War II came and went (George was shot down over Dresden, but survived), and the family began to drift apart. Becky Lee married my best friend, Brian Holtzman, and moved to Austin, MN, where they both secured positions at the Hormel (SPAM) plant. Agnes joined a circus trapeze act and traveled the country for sixteen years before shattering her hip in a nasty (twenty-foot) tumble. Zak's flower shop prospered when he landed several lucrative university contracts. Terri (severely retarded) remained at home with Mom and Pop. June moved to Bellingham, WA (pop. 45,794), and began a lucrative career as a fishing guide. Ike (Princeton educated) descended on Wall Street and made a million dollars before his 33rd birthday. Ezekial (slightly retarded) "went to Princeton" too, where he worked as a custodian for thirty-nine years. Karen, Penny, and George became "beatniks," traveling the country by rail for several years before eventually settling down (separately). They met Jack Kerouac in the spring of 1952, describing him as "exciting, but somewhat stuffy." Kim moved to Jasper, AR (pop. 519), where she married a wildly successful shoe-horn salesman, raising thirteen children of her own (all girls). Chris moved to St. Louis, MO where he soon landed a job as a "canner" at Chicken of the Sea Tuna. And then there's me! I moved to Houston, TX (pop. 4,876,003), where I worked at Uncle Ben's Rice for forty-two years.

It's been a wild, wonderful life! I'm seventy-eight years old, my wife (Agnes) and I have seen our two sons (Kip and Nat) raise several wonderful children of their own, and we've retired to gorgeous Colorado Springs (pop. 274, 318). Nine of my twelve brothers and sisters have passed on, but my life has been one of few regrets!

But I digress! If you put Arm & Hammer <u>Toothpaste</u> in your refrigerator, will it keep the foods from "polluting" each other...just like your baking soda? Also, could you send a (XL) T-shirt? Thanks, friends!

Food for thoughts,

Paul Rosa

Paul C. Rosa

CHURCH & DWIGHT CO., INC.
CONSUMER RELATIONS DEPARTMENT

469 NORTH HARRISON STREET P O BOX 7648
PRINCETON, N J. 08543-7648
1-609-683-5900
1-800-524-1328 1-800-624-2889 (N J)

November 5, 1993

Mr. Paul Rosa
P.O. Box 9368
Colo. Springs, CO 80932

Dear Mr. Rosa:

Thank you for taking the time to contact us regarding ARM & HAMMER® Toothpaste. We are pleased you enjoy using our product.

While you may find our product effective for deodorizing the refrigerator, we must caution you against this use. It is not intended for this purpose. Therefore, this application is considered misuse of product.

At ARM & HAMMER, we strive to manufacture products of high quality and performance which meet genuine consumer needs. We appreciate your patronage and have enclosed a sample of our NEW Baking Soda Fridge-Freezer Pack and a complimentary coupon for our Toothpaste. Also enclosed is literature providing uses for various ARM & HAMMER products.

Once again, thank you for contacting us. It's always nice to hear from satisfied consumers.

Cordially,

C. L. Collins

Christa L. Collins
Consumer Relations Representative

9300763210

P.O. Box 9368
Colo. Springs, CO 80932
September 21, 1993

Consumer Affairs
Budweiser Beer
Anheuser-Busch, Inc.
1 Busch Place
St. Louis, MO 63118-1849

Dear (Bud)dies,

There's nothing better than Budweiser Beer. Nothing. I've been drinking the delicious stuff since my 15th birthday, when my uncle (Crispin) bought me a case! Living in Lumberport, WV (pop. 939) as a young adult was no picnic, so my group of friends and I turned to Budweiser to "fill in the gap." I still remember the wild nights with my girlfriend (Becky Lee Holtzman) at the Mile-Hi Drive In, where we would watch scary movies and share can after can of your delicious beverage! She brought submarine sandwiches too.

Last year I moved to Colorado with my wife (Hanii) and two kids (Jud and Sue), and we prospered. I secured a job as a dog groomer while Hanii raked in the bucks as a respected cardiologist. Our combined income was soon over $200,000, so we could afford a lot of Budweiser. We routinely put away two or three (16 oz.) cases a week and our love flourished. Last spring we decided to invest in a built-in swimming pool, and as the workmen (Luke, Tim, Kip, Hans, and Agnes) finished the task, I had a crazy, beautiful idea!

I said to Hanii, "Why not fill the pool with beer, specifically Budweiser?" After initial reservations she countered, "Yes, why the hell not?" And our project was launched! We were soon hauling home van-loads of 16 ounce cases, and after two weeks we were done. We had purchased 13,000 cases (39,000 gallons of fluid), and spent about $235,000, but our 57° F *"refrigerated Bud pool"* was a reality! My wife and I jumped in (nude) and swam/drank under the stars. Let me assure you, it was heavenly! Soon our ("over 21") friends were invited and it's been party after party ever since. We have to replace about sixty cases a month, but hell, we've never been more popular! One night last week a dog fell into the pool and was found severely...plastered. The SPCA was enraged, but the dog's owner was soon comforted by a terrific, all-night party. Budweiser makes my life satisfying!

Anyway, I'm curious if this has been done before, and by whom. I'd be interested in corresponding with these folks and striking up friendships. Let me know, my friends!

Swimmin' and sippin',

Paul Rosa

Paul C. Rosa

P.S. Your Bud Bowl commercials crack me up (sheer genius)! *Also, I'd like a (XL) T-shirt!*

FLEISHMAN
HILLARD

Fleishman-Hillard, Inc.

Public Relations

February 8, 1994

200 North Broadway
St. Louis, Missouri 63102
Tel: 314.982.1700
Fax: 314.231.2313

Paul G. Koenig

Mr. Paul C. Rosa
P.O. Box 9368
Colo. Springs, CO 80932

Dear Mr. Rosa:

We enjoyed reading your letter and, as best we can tell, you're the only person we know who keeps the King of Beers in his swimming pool. Now that's dedication to Budweiser, the world's No. 1 brand!

Thanks, too, for your kind words about the Bud Bowl spots, and, of course, thanks for writing. Best regards for the new year, Mr. Rosa. It was good talking with you.

Sincerely,

Paul Koenig

Paul Koenig

PK/gs

P.O. Box 9368
Colo. Springs, CO 80932
September 21, 1993

Editorial Offices
Webster's New World Dictionary
850 Euclid Avenue
Cleveland, OH 44114

Dear Vocabulary Builders,

Congratulations on a superb product! Several times a day, when I'm at a loss for a particular word definition, I swiftly scamper to my den and consult Webster's New World Dictionary! Then I cheerfully return to my writing project (I'm working on a novel about the mating habits of Brazilian birds, and Simon & Schuster has already expressed interest!). *No one* should write without your trusty dictionary!

But before you strut triumphantly about your spacious editorial offices, thinking, "our product is absolutely without shortcomings," perhaps you should read on! Frankly, the book is too damn long (and heavy)! There are about 165,000 words in your dictionary, and many of them are **NEVER** used anymore. You could "trim the fat" by deleting many of these wasteful words, including the following "duds":

1. actinilite - a greenish type of amphibole.
2. bumph - official documents, regarded disparagingly.
3. elaterid - of the family of click beetles.
4. hagborn - having a hag or witch for a mother.
5. lobscouse - a sailor's stew of meat, vegetables, and hardtack.
6. mummer - a person who wears a mask or disguise for fun.
7. palinode - a poem written to retract something said in a previous poem.
8. quezal - same as Quetzal.
9. Virgil - a masculine name.
10. Zoug - former name of Zug.

These are just ten of the thousands of words that can be taken out to make the book more convenient and lighter. For instance, if you remove 8,250 words, the book should be 5% easier to use. If you can manage to discard 16,500 words, it'll be 10% easier to use, and, presumably, 10% lighter! It's an idea who's time has come, my well-spoken friends!

Please write to me with your thoughts on my proposed plan, and let me know some of the words *you* deem wasteful. Would you like me to send a longer list? I'm such a big fan of the English language that I'd be happy to contribute without compensation (though I wouldn't object to a *little* reimbursement!). I look forward to your swift reply! And I'd enjoy a (XL) T-shirt!

Hungry for lobscouse,

Paul Rosa

Paul C. Rosa

W E B S T E R ' S   N E W   W O R L D

Simon & Schuster Consumer Group
Citizens Building, Suite 306
850 Euclid Ave. '
Cleveland, OH 44114-3354
216-579-9970
Fax: 216-579-1255

Michael Agnes
Executive Editor

27 September 1993

Paul C. Rosa
P.O. Box 9368
Colo. Springs, CO 80932

Dear Mr. Rosa:

Thank you for your letter of 21 September and for your kind comments on our dictionaries.

I point out that college-level dictionaries for native speakers are designed primarily as decoding, or interpreting, dictionaries; that is, they are meant to explain words that are heard or read. We cannot remove the large number of entries you suggest because dictionary users still encounter such words when they read older literature.

Sincerely,

Michael Agnes

MEA:cs

A Paramount Communications Company

P.O. Box 9368
Colo. Springs, CO 80932
September 25, 1993

Consumer Affairs
Corporate Headquarters
Denver Broncos Football Team
13655 Broncos Parkway
Englewood, CO 80112

Dear Football Friends,

I'm a fifteen year old Bronco nut! My family has faithfully followed your terrific football team since November, 1972. We simply don't care that the Broncos have lost four Super Bowls, because it's *qualifying* for the big game that <u>really</u> counts! I'm sure a Super Bowl ring is in the cards, my friends. Just be patient. My Uncle Kermit is such a huge fan that he customized his car to look like a giant Broncos helmet (that's cool, don't you think?). My Grandma Agnes has died her hair orange and worn Bronco jerseys *to church* in the past. Yes, my family is just plain goofy, but they are wonderful, caring citizens. God bless them!

As an astute observer of sports in general, and football in particular, I have come up with some suggestions that would make your game better:

1. I've noticed that there have been some terrible injuries in recent years, and this should be addressed. Why not switch the game from "tackle" football to "touch" (or "flag") football? I bet this would decrease injuries by at least 75%, and few fans would object to the new format.
2. The field goal attempt is the most boring scenario in all of sports. I suggest you try "moving goal posts" that slide back and forth to make the dull situation more unpredictable.
3. Require each team to consist of at least 15% women. Sexism is no longer chic.
4. Change the shape of the playing field from a rectangle to a pentagon. It would add a new dimension (no pun intended) to the game and please military folks.
5. Every player should play every position (at least once) in each game. Now there's excitement!

Well, that's all for now, my friends! I'm currently doing a sophomore class project on my NFL Football improvements, and a reply from you would really help the report. Would you *please* write to me soon with your thoughts? Thank you so much!

Sports are vital,

Paul Rosa

Paul C. Rosa

P.S. Do you have any spare (XL) jerseys?

DEAR PAUL,

THANK YOU FOR WRITING.
YOU GIVE SOME VERY INTERESTING
SUGGESTIONS! I DON'T THINK THE
NFL IS LIKELY TO ADOPT THESE RIGHT
KNOW, BUT MAYBE SOME DAY THINGS
MIGHT CHANGE. TELL YOUR FAMILY
"THANK YOU" FOR THEIR SUPPORT +
THE BRONCOS ARE GLAD TO HAVE
SUCH TERRIFIC FANS!!

GOOD LUCK TO YOU,

Scott J. Dene
(P.R. ASSISTANT)

DENVER BRONCOS FOOTBALL CLUB
13655 BRONCOS PARKWAY   ENGLEWOOD, COLORADO 80112   (303) 649-9000
FAX (303) 649-9354

P.O. Box 9368
Colo. Springs, CO 80932
September 25, 1993

Customer Service
Pictionary, Incorporated
1200 Westlake North
Seattle, WA 98109

Dear Game Gang,

Pictionary is a blast!! I play about 300 games a year in the Southern Colorado Pictionary League (SCPL) with my pal, Agnes. So far this year our record is 176-32, and we're ranked second in the 30-35 age division. But we've already beaten the number one ranked team (Ray and Sylvia Corlis), so don't count us out yet, my friends!

When we play Pictionary just for fun (rarely), we sometimes add special rules to "spice up" the game a bit. I thought I'd share a few of them with you:

1. We use huge, thick magic-markers to make intricate drawing a virtual impossibility (we laugh for hours!).
2. We play "Reverse Strip Pictionary." Everyone begins the game naked, and when your team moves its piece the other team must each add an article of clothing. By the end of the game, the losers are sweating like war surgeons. Needless to say, it's a hoot!
3. We swap prescription eyeglasses so everything looks blurry (what a scream!).
4. Right-handed players must draw left-handed and left-handed players must draw right-handed (hysterical!).

So, you see, we know how to have fun! Some say that Pictionary is too important to me, but they (my selfish wife, Renee, among others) are just jealous! Congratulations on a wonderful product!

Finally, I want to share a disturbing dream I had last week. I dreamt I was playing Pictionary, and my drawing partner was **_Pablo Picasso_**. It was extremely frustrating, as his sketches were quite...unique. I was angrily shouting at him, "I don't know what it is!! A station wagon with three breasts and a war bonnet?! What _is_ it, damn it?!" I was about to punch him when Renee woke me up. Imagine, punching Pablo Picasso!

Isn't that a wild dream? Have you ever heard of such a thing? Do you think I may be playing too much Pictionary (I'd hate to admit Renee was right)? Do you offer any training manuals to improve one's skills? Is there a Pictionary newsletter? Do you have any (XL) T-shirts? Please let me know!
I look forward to your speedy response!

A man who thoroughly enjoys life ,

Paul Rosa

Paul C. Rosa

PICTIONARY
incorporated

October 7, 1993

Mr. Paul Rosa
P.O. Box 9368
Colo. Springs, CO 80932

Dear Paul,

Thank you for your recent letter to Pictionary Incorporated. We enjoy getting letters from Pictionary fans. Sounds like you have become very creative with your game play.

We hope this copy of "The Official Pictionary Dictionary" adds to your pleasure. Also, new on the market this fall is an updated for the '90s version of Pictionary.

Thanks again for the fun letter.

THE FOLKS AT PICTIONARY

P.O. Box 9368
Colo. Springs, CO 80932
September 29, 1993

Personnel
Caterpillar, Inc.
P.O. Box 1875
Peoria, IL 61656

Dear Caterpillar pillars of the community,

As an entomologist with 22 years of experience, I was *thrilled* when my co-worker (Agnes) told me about your terrific establishment! She explained that your tireless devotion to the larvae of butterflies and moths (caterpillars!) was the envy of Illinois, Indiana, Kentucky, Missouri, Iowa, and Wisconsin. As I am bored with my university lecturing position, I would like to explore the possibilities of doing research at your organization.

I received a Doctorate in Zoology from the University of Tennessee in the early 1970's -my transcripts are available to you upon request- and have devoted my life to insects ever since. But caterpillars have always been my passion! My personal favorites are those of the Lackey, Silkworm, Emperor Moth, and Hawk-moth. The caterpillars of the Hercules and Atlas Moths (with a wingspread of up to ten inches!) also rank among the most spectacular of the Lepidoptera. The larvae of the large swallowtail butterflies -with a hidden Y-shaped sac just behind their heads on the back of the thorax- are fascinating as well! I've always been impressed with the delicate and orderly way caterpillars eat (precise snipping at the edge of a leaf). Even in their excrement, healthy caterpillars are inoffensive, and a special term 'frass' is used to describe the little dry pellets which are welcome evidence that their appetite and digestion are in good order. Their transformations into butterflies are glorious to follow and....wait a minute!

I don't know why I've been rambling on and on about caterpillars when you folks are clearly the experts! I guess it's tough to stop me once I'm "on a roll!" I would, however, like to hear about the available opportunities at your terrific institute (museum?). Do you have enough entomologists at this time or are you interviewing fresh faces? I would bring a lifetime of love and respect (for the caterpillar) to my new job, and would relish the chance to return to my home state. Raised in charming Dixon, IL (pop. 15,659), I have only glorious memories! Please do what you can to make my homecoming a reality! I look forward to a quick response, my friends. By the way, did you know "caterpillar" comes from the Latin words "catta" and "pilosa," meaning "hairy cat?" I <u>knew</u> you did!!

Peacock Butterflies are nice too!

Paul Rosa

Dr. Paul C. Rosa

P.S. How about a (XL) T-shirt for my ambitious son, Ed? He'd be grateful!

CATERPILLAR®

Caterpillar Inc.

100 NE Adams Street
Peoria, Illinois 61629

February 9, 1994

Dr. Paul C. Rosa
P.O. Box 9368
Colo. Springs, CO 80932

Dear Dr. Rosa:

I am sorry for the delay in answering your inquiry concerning employment with Caterpillar Inc. Your background is commendable and your devotion to the larvae of butterflies and moths is very commendable. However, this dedication is not one which we endeavor to employ.

I have routed your request for employment to different academia in the Peoria area to see if they know of some type of employment for individuals who have studied the Hercules and Atlas moths. I am sorry to say I could generate no interest in your behalf.

Finally, you will note that although your formal education in zoology is commendable, it is not fitting for the type of business that Caterpillar Inc. is involved in. To help explain what I mean, I'm enclosing for your information the brochure explaining Caterpillar and its products.

Again, may I commend you on your seeking employment in a very fine disciplinary area and wish you the best in securing what I would imagine would be a very interesting and yet peculiar area of study.

Sincerely,

C. A. Williams

Manager
Professional & Technical Employment

CAWilliams
Telephone: (309) 675-4279
js\caw\rosa

Enc.

P.O. Box 9368
Colo. Springs, CO 80932
October 2, 1993

Ms. Penny Bost, Manager
Chapel Hills 9 Movie Theater
The Chapel Hills Mall
1710 Briargate Blvd.
Colo. Springs, CO 80920

Dear Movie Maestro,

I've seen many terrific movies at your facility over the years, featuring such talented stars as
Sylvester Stallone, Jean Claude Van Damme, Tom Selleck, and the daughter of Francis Ford
Coppola (Agnes?). Your fine film offerings and terrific snacks (Milk-Duds, wieners,
popcorn with "butter flavoring," etc.) have made for some memorable outings. My wife, Jen,
and I are thankful for your efforts. Keep up the good work, my friend!

But we're not 100% satisfied and thought you should know why. Recently we were at your
theater, watching a movie featuring Robert DeNiro or Jodie Foster, or some other overrated
"star." Halfway through the presentation we grew fiercely bored and vacated the premises.
Several months later (now) we realized how unfair that situation was. We paid full price for
half of a movie! Ms. Bost, that's simply not the American way, damn it (forgive the
profanity)!

Why not follow the lead of your adult theater counterparts? Customers should have the option
of inserting quarters into a slot until the movie is no longer intriguing to them. When the
quarters "stop," the seats could grow extremely hot, thus thwarting cheaters. Alternatively, the
quarters could halt the progress of a sharp spike which would slowly rise from the seat. If Al
Pacino or Glenn Close are (predictably) sub-par, customers could exit quietly, perhaps having
lost only $1.25 apiece. It's an idea who's time has come, ma'am!

Please *write* to me with your thoughts on my ground-breaking idea (phone calls are so
impersonal!). Also, let me know if Brooke Shields is "coming" to your theater soon. Since
"Blue Lagoon," she has apparently fallen off the face of the earth, and this movie fan (among
others) misses her! And what about Marvin Hagler? I look forward to a swift response and
(if available) a complimentary (XL) T-shirt!

Down in front,

Paul Rosa

Paul C. Rosa

P.S. What are the ingredients of "butter flavoring?"

Carmike Cinemas

October 8, 1993

Paul Rosa
P.O. Box 9368
Colo. Springs, CO 80932

Dear Down in Front:

Wow! It's really amazing how many movies you have truly seen at our facility. We've enjoyed having you as a customer throughout the years and hope all the "talented" stars you've observed on our giant screen have filled many happy hours for you. But, Paul, eating wieners, milk duds and butter flavoring all in one trip can really cause your insides to do flip flops and cause a drastic fluctuation in your dietary waste. That was probably not a smart decision you made. I was sorry to hear, however, that you only watched half of the movie you paid full price for. (You should learn never to pay full price for a movie when you can go to a matinee or just sneak in.) I've enclosed two passes to make up for the bad DeNiro movie that you saw. Hopefully, you'll be a little wiser with your next choice.

Your idea about inserting quarters to keep the movie going was quite an interesting one. However, using this idea movies could get quite expensive. Such features as "Dances with Wolves" could cost upwards of ten dollars due to the length, whereas children's movies, such as Aladdin, would be quite inexpensive. There would be no fair way of generating equal amounts of revenue. The disadvantages of these types of seats, I think, would outweigh the advantages. Think of the cost involved in remodeling each auditorium and the sacrifice of comfort (due to the spike sticking out of each seat.) Maybe you should approach the film companies themselves to help in the cost of the remodeling. Maybe they would start making quality features to keep the quarters coming in.

I'm sorry we can't help you out with the quarter idea, but we hate to think of our competition as the adult theatres who do such things. As far as T-Shirts go we don't have any. Sorry!

Sincerely,

The Movie Maestro
Penny Bost

P.S. Butter flavoring contains "partially hydrogenated soybean oil with TBHQ and citric acid added to preserve freshness, dimethylpolysiloxane added to reduce foaming, no water, beta carotene added for color, and artificial flavor."

P.O. Box 9368
Colo. Springs, CO 80932
October 2, 1993

Gerald S. Stein, M.D., Psychiatrist
1415 N. Cascade Ave.
Colorado Springs, CO 80907

Dear Dr. Stein,

You don't know me, but maybe you should. I'm a young man with a hobby that many would consider odd. I write approximately five letters a week to corporations all over America, from the perspective of an idiot. Here are some samples, my friend:

- I wrote to the Caterpillar Corporation, asking them if they were currently hiring any entomologists.
- I wrote to a retirement home, asking if I could live there, as I love the elderly.
- I contacted a local pastor, asking if I could have his "old" holy water for my water bed.
- I wrote to Johnson & Johnson Dental Floss, angrily pointing out that their "100 yard roll" was, in fact, somewhat shorter than that.

Well, what do you think? Is there reason for concern? Furthermore, when I write these letters I assume other people's identities. For instance, when I wrote to the Caterpillar Corporation, I "felt" like Lucille Ball. As I hammered away at my computer keyboard, I shrieked at my "husband," Ricki. When I typed the letter to the pastor, I took on the persona of Mahatma Gandhi and didn't eat for two days. Is this okay? Is there a name for my condition? Is it my mother's fault? My father's? Can I make money doing this? Also, if I am to come in for treatment, I would like to know some things first:

1. Is your furniture non-leather? I'm a strict PETA (People for the Ethical Treatment of Animals) member!
2. Do you provide free Kleenex? Is it scented?
3. Are patients permitted to come to the office covered with cheese slices?
4. Is good hygiene a must? I bathe only twice monthly.
5. May patients bring house pets? I have a cat (Agnes) who accompanies me everywhere.

As I heard you were one of the best psychiatrists in north-central Colorado Springs, I felt it would be wise to contact you. Please write (I have no phone) and let me know your thoughts. I look forward to a quick response! And please send a (XL) T-shirt. God bless.

Freud was cool,

Paul Rosa

Paul C. Rosa

GERALD S. STEIN, M.D., P.C.

PSYCHOANALYSIS
PSYCHIATRY

1415 NORTH CASCADE AVENUE
COLORADO SPRINGS, CO 80907
(719) 636-2280

October 6, 1993

Paul C. Rosa
P.O. Box 9368
Colo. Springs, CO 80932

Dear Mr. Rosa,

As a leading spokesman for mental health in north-central Colorado Springs, I have given your letter of October 2nd, and its question of whether you should be concerned and seek professional help considerable thought. I have concluded that it is not your mental health which is in need of shoring up, but your confidence that your hobby, while it is not in the mainstream, is indicative of unusual strength and creativity.

The capacity to see multiple meanings in conventional terms like the Caterpillar Corporation exponentially expands your world.

Being able to feel what it might be like to be something other than yourself, such as an elderly individual, a woman, or even Mahatma Gandhi, attests to the flexibility of a more protean identity, instead of a rigid, brittle identity so vulnerable in changing circumstances.

Your hobby also seems to have helped consolidate a new and deeper sense of identity which should encourage you to proceed with more confidence and compete more effectively in a world where so few have a deep sense of identity.

My confidence in your advanced state is also good news for me. Trying to treat you and get that cheese off my leather chairs would drive me up the wall.

Sincerely,

Gerald S. Stein, M.D.

P.O. Box 9368
Colo. Springs, CO 80932
October 2, 1993

Personnel Department
Time Magazine, Inc.
Time & Life Building
Rockefeller Center
New York, NY 10020-1393

Hello fellow writers,

I have been a subscribber to your Time magazine for almost ten or elleven months now and
I think it would be a really great job to be someone who gets to write for your great magazine for a
living! I'm 31 years old and I work in Colorado as a dog groomer but my friends keep on telling me
that I would make a good writer and should try and get a job at a magazine or writing a book or
something like it!

I took some journalism classes when I went to high school in Alachua, FL (pop. 3561), and my
teacher always said I was really pretty good with my words and should try to write some more than I
was doing then at that time. After high school I went to a community college for five months, but
had to drop out when my girlfriend (Becky Lee Agnesman) went and got herself pregnant with me.
I wanted to own up to what I'd done, so I got a job working with my daddy in a pulp mill on the
other side of town. I have been a good father with my daughter, but my dream of someday being a
writer who gets to get paid for his writing is a dream that has never went away in all the years.

Last week, my coeworker, Bo, said I should stop talking about doing the writing and start doing
something about that writing. I figured he was right, and I'm not getting any younger, so I thought it
might be a really good idea that I should get in touch with you and ask you to please send me an
application for working. I wouldn't mind starting out as a junior reporter or something, but I'd be
lieing if I said that I didn't want to be a reporter who took care of the biggest stories like the one
about that train going into the river down there in Louisiana one night last month. That was a
terrible thing, and I figured I could write some really good things about it and make everyone feel
sorry for what happened and all that. I even bought me a computer so as I could be a better writer
than I was before I bought it!

So are you doing some hiring nowadays? How often do you interview writers like me that want to
write as reporters at Time magazine? I would be happy to come out at anytime and give you an
interview so you can tell if I'd be good working there. I'm looking forward to you getting in touch
with me soon and telling me what the job posibilities are there with you. Thanks for your help with
my dream! And could you send a XL T-shirt? God bless!

I'll talk to you all soon,

Paul Rosa

Paul C. Rosa

Personnel Department
Time Magazine, Inc.
Time & Life Building
Rockefeller Center
New York, NY 10020-1393

Dear Hiring Department,

Say now, it's been over five weeks since I wrote to you all, asking if you where hiring writers like me. I explained to you that I have read Time magazine for almost a year now and think that I would be very good at writing for you. I explained that my fiend Bo thought I should stop talking about the writing and actually try to get a job doing that writing! It wasn't easy to write my first letter (October 2), but I did it, expecting that you could tell me your answer and feelings about me real quickly. I have been real disappointed that you haven't written in five weeks and really feel like you are hurting my feelings or something like it.

But then I got to thinking and figured you maybe lost my letter in the mail room or it fell under the carpet or something. I once lost a baseball cap of mine and didn't find it again for a month because it got stuck under the seat in my truck. But boy was I happy when I found it! So I know how these things do happen and I wanted to give you all another chance at reading my letter, so I'm sending the first one again with a stamped envelope to make it all easier. I'd really like it if you could finally think it over about my becoming a writer at Time and give me a QUICK answer in the envelope.

I just finished reading about your recent cover story on Cloning Humans and think folks are meddling with the work that God is supposed to be doing. If I had reported on this story I would have mentioned that and given a pretty good opinion from a fella who was raised in a Christian house where we had proper respect for women and babies and things. So please write to me right away and let me know if your hiring writers and let me know what I should do next like send some samples or something. Please don't hurt my feelings again by not sending a letter because it's hard to be hurt you know. Thank you very much! God bless.

Time magazine is #1,

Paul Rosa

Paul C. Rosa

212-522-1212

Time Inc.

November 17, 1993

Mr. Paul C. Rosa
P.O. Box 9368
Colo. Springs, CO 80932

Dear Mr. Rosa:

This will acknowledge and thank you for your recent letter expressing interest in employment opportunities within the Time Inc.

Our recruiters will review your qualifications in light of our current staffing needs and will contact you for an interview should an opening occur which would be commensurate with your experience and interests. If we do not have a suitable opportunity available, your resume will be retained in our file for reference against future needs.

In the interim, you have our best wishes for success in your career search and our sincere thanks for your interest in Time Inc.

Sincerely,

Stephanie Mack

Stephanie Mack
Human Resources
/sm

P.O. Box 9368
Colo. Springs, CO 80932
October 3, 1993

Ms. Oprah Winfrey
HARPO, Inc.
110 N. Carpenter St.
Chicago, IL 60607

Dear Ms. Winfrey ("Oprah" is probably for friends only),

I was pleased to hear that you were the highest paid entertainer of 1992. $95,000,000 is a
nice chunk of change, and is probably more than most <u>communities</u> in North Dakota will
make in a (collective) lifetime! I made about $13,250 last year as a dog groomer and
thought I was doing okay. Then I look at *your* accomplishment and realize I'm pretty lame!
At this rate I would have to work for 7,170 years to equal what your earn in *one year*!
Geez, you earn more *every eighteen minutes* (based on a 40 hour week) than I do all year!
You are truly living the American dream.

I would enjoy taking a year off from work and traveling around the country with my
girlfriend, Bonnie. Since an eighteen minute (.30 hours) effort for you brings in about
$13,702, I was hoping you could "devote" your salary for this brief time interval to us just
once! If you sent me a check for the aforementioned amount, Bonnie and I could leave for
California and "find ourselves." We could also explore Arizona, Florida, New England,
Missouri, Montana, Alaska, and Hawaii. We'll probably never be able to afford this on our
own (Bonnie doesn't work), so we thought you would be glad to help. Eighteen minutes
isn't so much, is it? Or perhaps you'd be more comfortable with a round number like thirty
minutes ($22,837). It's up to you, of course.

Please get back to me soon and let me know what you think of my idea. I know you're
busy lining up fascinating guests and have little patience for letter writing, but I hoped an
exception would be made in our case. You are truly a remarkable woman! God bless!

With calculator in hand,

Paul Rosa

Paul C. Rosa

P.S. Please send a (XL) T-shirt for Bonnie.

OPRAH
THE OPRAH WINFREY SHOW

October 19, 1993

Mr Paul Rosa
P.O. Box 9368
Colo. Springs, CO 80932

Dear Mr Rosa,

Thank you for writing and letting us know you watch **The Oprah Winfrey Show.**

Oprah receives an overwhelming number of requests similar to yours and although she is unable to accommodate them all, please know that she wishes you the best.

Sincerely,

Correspondent
The Oprah Winfrey Show

SB:mq

P.O. Box 9368
Colo. Springs, CO 80932
October 3, 1993

Personnel Department
The Mayo Clinic
200 1st St., SW
Rochester, MN 55902

Dear Sandwich Sultans,

When I heard about your exclusive institute from my grandmother (Erma), I almost shrieked with pleasure! You see, for *years* I have searched for the perfect mayonnaise recipe and sadly thought I was alone in my passionate pursuit! To learn that there actually exists a facility that devotes *all* of its resources to perfecting this delicious condiment is truly wonderful. At first I didn't believe Erma, but my neighbor (Agnes) confirmed her story and gladly gave me your address. I am overjoyed to write to you!

My interest in mayonnaise began in 1967, as a young lad growing up in McIntosh, ND (pop. 4,800). My mother (Rachel) would routinely mix a dollop of Kraft mayonnaise with several ounces of Chicken of the Sea (old fisherman name for White Albacore) tuna fish, spreading it on white bread. I would fairly attack the sandwich, consuming it in several ravenous bites. Then I would dash outside and join my best friends (Lenny, Sam, and Glenn) at the city park, where we played "kick the can" and other character-building games. Those were the happiest days of my life, my friends! But I digress!

My love for mayonnaise grew throughout my teenage years, reaching its zenith when I enjoyed turkey and mayonnaise sandwiches with my best gal (Becky Lee Holtzagnes) after our senior prom in 1980. I also lost my virginity that night, but this topic requires a separate letter! At the University of Budapest (exchange program) I majored in Chemistry and Food Service, devoting much of my time to mayonnaise experimentation. During my junior year (1983), I created a concoction featuring ordinary mayonnaise, parsley, cinnamon, and mustard. The result was extraordinary, and many of the Hungarian cafeterias still feature my delicious find. I was clever enough to "patent" the mix, so I have earned a tidy sum (mid six figures) from my "Mayonnaise Delight!" I haven't been able to equal this accomplishment since, but I continue to tirelessly work in my lab.

Are you hiring any scientists at *your* labs? You won't find a harder working person who is more devoted to mayonnaise. My family (Becky Lee and the triplets Zak, Zeba, and Tristan) would have no problem moving, and I would welcome the chance to live in Minnesota. I understand the climate and citizens are terrific. Please get back to me immediately and let me know the job prospects. I anxiously await your reply! And please send a (XL) T-shirt.

No ketchup for me,

Paul Rosa

Paul C. Rosa

Mayo Clinic

Rochester, Minnesota 55905   Telephone 507 284-2511

Personnel Section

Dear Applicant:

We have received your correspondence and appreciate your consideration of Mayo Clinic Rochester as a prospective employer.

Unfortunately, you have not been selected for an interview at this time. We will keep your correspondence on file for three months and if an opportunity should develop during that time, we will contact you again.

Thank you for your interest in Mayo. We wish you well in your pursuit of a challenging employment opportunity.

MAYO CLINIC
PERSONNEL SECTION

P.O. Box 9368
Colo. Springs, CO 80932
October 3, 1993

Consumer Affairs
Friskies Cat Food Company
Glendale, CA 91203

Dear Feline Fanciers,

My name is Jesse and I am a black (African-American?) cat. For eleven years (77 to you) my "owner," Paul has faithfully fed me delicious portions of Friskies canned food, and I thought it was time to send a letter of appreciation! For the past four months, while Paul slept, I secretly learned how to use his word processor. Since I have no opposable claws, writing utensils simply weren't an option! But I'm clearly no dummy!

Life in Colorado has been very pleasant. In my younger years I kept myself busy by joyfully slaughtering scores of small animals (mice, birds, etc.) and exploring the vast neighborhood. My mating urges were eliminated early on by a procedure I really can't remember. Let me tell you though, it took a while to forgive Paul for that one! My energy level was always high, since I received many cans of Friskies and plenty of water (milk gives me the runs). In 1986 (age 4 or 28) I was hit by a car which broke my leg and pissed me off (the bastard was speeding). For a month I was unable to go outside and had to wear a ridiculous Elizabethan collar to prevent me from licking the wound. I bet that Elizabeth was a bitch (female dog)!

In my "middle years," I slowed down a bit, but still managed to kill my share of miserable, little neighborhood creatures. In 1991 (age 9 or 63) I had the zest to bring down a pheasant! It fought like a champion, but I eventually managed to snap its neck like an autumn twig! The delicious portions of Friskies -my favorite is Turkey & Giblets- continued to arrive in my bowl, and I felt warm and loved! Then in 1992 Paul met a woman (Agnes Holtzman) who soon moved in with him/us! I was irate at first, but it turns out that she is one cool lady! She "sneaks" me extra portions of Friskies, and I am happily easing off the hunting schedule, opting for leisurely days on the sofa instead. Agnes likes to brush me too, and this makes me feel great all over! And she cleans out my litter box regularly, something Paul apparently finds frivolous. I never thought I'd welcome a stranger into my place, but I guess you *can* teach an old cat new tricks! Don't ask me to "fetch" though, unless *you* have nine lives!

Well, it's 1993 and I'm a "senior cat," looking forward to many more happy years. The Friskies have been a vital part of my life, and I hope you keep up the superb work, my friends! I was also wondering if you need any help testing cat food. Perhaps you could send some new flavors for me to try and I could report back via the word processor! Also, if you could send a (XL) T-shirt for Paul, I'm sure he'd be thrilled! Write soon and God bless!

Always landing on my feet,

Paul Rosa

Jesse (the cat) Rosa

I ♣ my dog!

Friskies.

Friskies PetCare Company

Office of Consumer Affairs
800 North Brand Boulevard
Glendale, CA 91203
Telephone: (818) 549-6818

Author's Note: Jesse is a lady!

1993

Mr. Jesse (the cat) Rosa
P.O. Box 9368
Colo. Springs, CO 80932

Dear Mr. Rosa:

Thank you for taking the time to write to us about Friskies dry cat food. We appreciate your kind and thoughtful comments.

All Friskies PetCare products are carefully formulated and tested for performance and palatability at our research facilities. Generations of dogs and cats have been successfully fed an exclusive diet of our products. Compliments like yours help us feel that we are achieving our goal of providing the highest quality pet foods available.

We value you as a customer and trust that we will continue to merit your confidence and loyalty.

Sincerely,

Chris Cappiello

Chris Cappiello
Consumer Correspondent

1959 101993 PASADENA

GLENDALE
OCT 19 '93
CA

≡0.29≡
PB METER
7000261   U.S. POSTAGE

Friskies.

Friskies PetCare Company

Office of Consumer Affairs
800 North Brand Blvd.
Glendale, CA   0372584A3 / 2244

Mr. Jesse (the cat) Rosa
P.O. Box 9368
Colo. Springs, CO 80932

P.O. Box 9368
Colo. Springs, CO 80932
October 4, 1993

Consumer Concerns
CITGO Gasoline Company
P.O. Box 992
Tulsa, OK 74102

Dear Fuel Fellas,

I was reading Parade Magazine on Sunday -it is the best damn one on the market- when I saw your ad in there. I sent a copy of it which I made at the duplicating place up the road a spell. I thought it was a nice photograph of one of your gas stations until I spotted the biggest damn eagle I ever seen about to land on the roof! That bird looks like it must be about 13 foot high with a wing span of over 30 foot! I'll bet it scared that photographer fella half to death (if he survived). Now I seen my share of eagles in my time in Colorado and Nebraska and Wyoming, but I never seen one that was near as big as this one is!

As a hard working rancher who has about 70 head of cattle, I need to know where this picture was taken! If these eagles are flying around Colorado, I'll bet they'd have no problem eating a cow or two of mine. I've got a few guns in my house, but it would take a cannon to stop that bastard! Has the government been told about this bird? Are there more than one? Do they ever go after people? My wife (Agnes) is so scared, she won't walk around outside without looking up all the time. I keep telling her that these eagles are probably in Alaska or something where all the biggest animals are, but I'm not so sure!

Please write to me real fast and let me know more about this gigantic animal. My brother, Ben in Culbertson, Montana (pop. 887) is waiting to hear about your letter too. Them government snot noses probably already have the critter on the endangered list, but if it comes near my ranch I'll open fire with everything I got. And you can take that to the bank!

Always buy American,

Paul Rosa

Paul C. Rosa

P.S. Do you have a (XL) T-shirt for my oldest son, Burt?

CITGO Petroleum Corporation

P.O. Box 3758
Tulsa OK 74102-3758

November 16, 1993

Mr. Paul C. Rosa
P.O. Box 9368
Colo. Springs, CO 80932

Dear Mr. Rosa:

Please put your fears to rest and your gun back in its holster. The giant eagles that have been appearing in our ads are well-trained and live in captivity so, barring an escape, they should never darken the skies over your Colorado ranch. If, however, one should slip its tether, we will notify you immediately so you, Agnes and your brother Ben can take the appropriate precautions.

Thank you for taking the time to bring your concerns to our attention. Although we do apologize for causing any undo panic, we're pleased to know that our unique approach to photography was indeed eye-catching and memorable.

In fact, those of us here at CITGO's headquarters enjoyed your comments so much, we shared your letter with more than 2,000 employees and guests at our recent distributor meeting in Scottsdale, Arizona. Mr. Rosa, you were quite a hit.

To show our appreciation to you and your fine sense of humor (or incredibly active imagination...whichever the case may be) we did find an XL t-shirt for your son, Burt, and also enclosed a few gifts for you. We hope you enjoy them and we also hope you won't hesitate to stop by a CITGO station for a fill-up. Trust us. It should be safe.

Sincerely,

Larry H. Brittain, Jr.
Vice President
Marketing

*3
T-Shirts
Received!!!*

P.O. Box 9368
Colo. Springs, CO 80932
October 8, 1993

U.S. Flag Commission
The White House
1600 Pennsylvania Ave.
Washington, DC 20500

Dear Patriots (not New England!),

I've always proudly displayed an 8' x 4' American flag on my front porch (365 days a year), and that was never more important than when my boy, Oscar, served in the Persian Gulf conflict. As the fighting in Kuwait raged, I comforted myself by gently wrapping a smaller flag around my shoulders and reciting the pledge of allegiance over and over again. The flag continues to be an important part of my life, even as the very fabric of our country crumbles around us! Drive-by shootings, global warming, and the eroding acting skills of Marlon Brando are just a few of the indignities we are forced to endure on a regular basis!

Something has troubled me for seven weeks, and I thought you might be able to ease my mind. I've always been comfortable with the design of the American flag until recently. I am pleased that the thirteen stripes are present, to honor the original thirteen colonies. I am also content with the fifty stars which represent the fifty states. What I <u>don't</u> approve of, is the *size* of these stars! The star for Wyoming (pop. 515,000) is the same size as California's (pop. 30,000,000)! Is this fair? The same "star size" which represents 550,000 citizens (Vermont) shouldn't *also* represent 20,000,000 folks (New York)! That's ludicrous!

What I am recommending is a fair solution! The less populated states (Wyoming, Vermont, North Dakota, Montana, etc.) should have smaller stars than California, New York, Texas, Pennsylvania, etc. The stars of states like Indiana and Georgia, with populations of approximately 6,000,000 (about average), would barely be altered. Under my plan, since many states would have smaller stars and many would have larger ones, the total *space* required for stars on the flag would be unchanged. Colorado's star size would be reduced by about 42% (our population is 3,500,000), so I am clearly not pursuing this for selfish reasons. It simply pains me to see some people "more represented" than others on the flag. That's not the democratic way!

So, what do you think of my idea? If this plan is instituted, am I eligible for an award (key to the city)? Lastly, do you have (XL) T-shirts? Please respond <u>quickly</u>, my friends.

Home of the brave,

Paul Rosa

Paul C. Rosa

P.S. Changing the "thickness" of the flag stripes is a good idea too (letter to follow)!

THE WHITE HOUSE

WASHINGTON

December 17, 1993

Mr. Paul C. Rosa
P.O. Box 9368
Colo. Springs, CO 80932

Dear Paul:

I appreciate your taking the time to write.

It's important for me to hear the thoughts and experiences
of people who care about the future of America and the world. We
face many challenges ahead, and in order for us to come together
and build consensus, we all must share our ideas and concerns.

I look forward to your support as we tackle the issues
facing us in the coming months.

Sincerely,

P.O. Box 9368
Colo. Springs, CO 80932
October 7, 1993

Advertising Department
Wheaties Cereal c/o General Mills, Inc.
Number One General Mills Boulevard
Golden Valley, MN 55426

Dear Whole Grain Goodness Gods,

I've been wolfing down bowls of Wheaties since I was a skinny, young lad growing up on the mean streets of Brooklyn (huge population)! Whenever the neighborhood bullies (Russ and Kurt) would beat me up, my mother would soothe me by gently offering a delicious bowl of your super cereal. The whole grain goodness helped me reach 200 pounds of muscle by my 17th birthday, and I still proudly remember the day (May 16, 1978) that I clobbered Russ and Kurt *simultaneously*! I can't thank your company enough!

I was rather saddened by the news of Michael Jordan's retirement. With a few possible exceptions (Wayne Gretzky, Nolan Ryan, Carl Lewis, Martina Navratilova, and Pele), he is the greatest athlete on the face of the planet. I'll never forget the way he soared through the air for what seemed like a long time, before tossing the perfect pass to one of his delighted teammates on the field of play. He also appeared the complete gentleman, always taking the time to speak to a child or offering to help the community with his efforts! Let's all take a moment and mourn the passing of a great man from the public's (sometimes cruel) eye!

Since Michael appeared regularly on the cover of your Wheaties boxes, I assume you are looking for suitable substitutes. Without further ado, I offer my list of suggestions, along with the reasons:

- Kurt Russell - Terrific actor, married to Goldie Hawn.
- Al Gore - Vice President, handsome man.
- Sally Struthers - Humanitarian, Archie's daughter.
- Billie Jean King - Bobby Riggs' nemesis.
- Paul Reubens ("Pee Wee Herman") - To forgive is divine.
- Kris Kristofferson - Country singer, etc.

I have some more ideas if you'd like to hear them. I'd also like to know why, in TV commercials, cereal is always depicted with milk *splashing* onto it, then out of the bowl. It seems so messy (and wasteful). I look forward to your swift response to my above suggestions and this question. I'd also appreciate a (XL) T-shirt, my friends. God bless!

No eggs for me,

Paul Rosa

Paul C. Rosa

P.O. Box 9368
Colo. Springs, CO 80932
November 22, 1993

Advertising Department
Wheaties Cereal c/o General Mills, Inc.
Number One General Mills Boulevard
Golden Valley, MN 55426

Dear Cereal Chieftains,

Say now, it's been over six weeks (October 7, 1993) since I wrote to you with my suggestions for celebrities to put on your Wheaties boxes. Since Michael Jordan has shockingly retired, I assume that you are looking for suitable (or at least semi-suitable) replacements. Let's face it, an athlete of such talents and charisma comes along as often as Haley's Comet. But my Uncle Kent always said, "If you get lemons, make lemonade!" He took credit for that line, but I think it's been around far longer than he has (67 years). By ignoring my letter for 46 days, I feel like *you've* given me lemons, but by writing again I am attempting to make lemonade. I don't even like lemonade -I drink Dr. Pepper- but the spirit of the saying remains intact. Alas, I'm meandering...

I have good-naturedly chosen to re-submit a copy of my original letter *and* a self-addressed, stamped envelope to make the (apparently) overwhelming task of responding to a faithful consumer a bit easier. Forgive my sarcasm, but when a man purchases 500 (or so) boxes of a product from a corporation, he expects to be treated with distinction! Since I have some space left on this page, I have trustingly chosen to submit a few more ideas for the cover of your cereal boxes. I hope I'm not wasting my time again, but I've always maintained that all people are basically good. So, without further ado, here are my (second) suggestions:

     ♫ Ben Franklin - Patriot, electricity expert.
     ♫ Old Yeller - Legendary canine.
     ♫ Flip Wilson - Remember "Geraldine?" Hilarious.
     ♫ Bob Dole - Incorruptible Kansas politician.
     ♫ King Ludwig of Bavaria - He was wonderfully eccentric.
     ♫ The Bee Gees - Have the second-highest selling album in history.
     ♫ Barney the Dinosaur - Purple and lovable!

Well, that's all for now. I would *really* appreciate it if you could finally get back to me with a thorough discussion of my suggestions. I'm a busy electrician who has little energy for pursuing unresponsive companies. Your time is appreciated, my friends! Be well.

Always eager to pitch in,

Paul Rosa

Paul C. Rosa

General Mills, Inc.
General Offices

Post Office Box 1113
Minneapolis, Minnesota 55440

December 3, 1993

Mr. Paul C. Rosa
P.O. Box 9368
Colo. Springs, CO 80932

Dear Mr. Rosa:

Thank you for your letters of October 7, 1993 and November 22, 1993. They have come to me for reply because all letters offering suggestions are sent to this department. Apparently, your October 7, 1993 letter was misplaced which explains why you never received a response and for this I apologize.

A great many of our consumer friends comment on our advertising and promotional materials, those in and on our boxes, in magazines or newspapers, or on our television programs, etc. A number of them, like you, suggest either changes or additional examples they would like us to use. We note your request that we picture celebrities such as Kurt Russell, Billie Jean King, Ben Franklin, Barney the Dinosaur, etc. on the front of WHEATIES boxes.

<u>While we do not solicit suggestions now offer compensation for them</u>, we do want to offer products, packages and advertising that will meet the desires and interests of our customers. So, when a suggestion is offered on a helpful basis without obligation of any kind, we are happy to pass it along to appropriate personnel for their guidance in providing such products, packages or advertising. We are enclosing a return postcard on which you may confirm your wishes. If you sign and return the card, you may be sure that we will register your vote to picture celebrities such as Kurt Russell, Billie Jean King, Ben Franklin, Barney the Dinosaur, etc. on the front of WHEATIES boxes.

Our Betty Crocker Kitchens have many suggestions for our products, and we are enclosing some recipes we hope you will enjoy using.

Again, thank you for writing.

Sincerely,

Linda Belisle

Linda E. Belisle
Paralegal-Submitted Ideas

LEB
Enclosure

P.O. Box 9368
Colo. Springs, CO 80932
October 8, 1993

Mr. Peter Widdrington
Commissioner of Major League Baseball
350 Park Ave.
New York 10022

Dear national pastime preserver,

Thanks for your help in the clever decision to break up the two leagues (National and American) into three divisions apiece. Let's face it, baseball has become as stale as my Grandma Policky's French bread. Your new format will give this sport the shot of adrenaline it so desperately needs to compete in this "thrill a minute" world we call earth! By the way, how about calling the championship, "Earth Series?" It's colorful, isn't it?

Yes, six divisions and two wild-card teams are certainly steps in the right direction, but other changes would be embraced as well. A typical game now consists of perhaps fifteen minutes of true action in a three hour period! That's not enough, for God's sake! After formulating a number of solutions with my Pictionary buddies (Rusty, Sue, Tim, Beth, and Clem), we voted on the best ones, and I offer them now for your review:

- Fewer players on defense! With only four or five fielders, offenses would explode!
- Move the pitcher's mound back twenty feet and watch the batting averages (and stadium attendances) soar!
- Coat random areas of the field with a slippery substance, like PAM Cooking Spray. Everyone enjoys a good laugh at someone else's expense!
- One less base would increase scoring by about 14%! This would also allow several hundred more <u>paying</u> fans in the stadium. And triangles *look* nicer than diamonds!
- Once each game, pick (at random) a lucky fan to bat. After all, it *is* the fans' game!
- Prohibit the (usually portly) managers from wearing team uniforms. All the other major sports have wisely already done so. Tight uniforms aren't for the sedentary!
- No more relief pitchers. This reduces the exciting scoring fans crave!
- Permit two defensive "tackles" per game.

We came up with many more ideas, but would like to hear your input on these first, my friend! Also, could you tell me how one becomes an umpire? I am a huge man with a Herculean voice, so I'd be perfect for the job! Does it pay well? Lastly, do you have any (XL) T-shirts? I look forward to your swift reply, sir. God bless you.

Pardon Pete!

Paul Rosa

Paul C. Rosa

December 8, 1993

Mr. Paul C. Rosa
P.O. Box 9368
Colo. Springs, CO 80932

Dear Mr. Rosa:

Peter Widdrington asked me to respond to your recent letters. I apologize for the delays.

While your proposals are interesting, if implemented they would result in a game barely resembling baseball as we know it today. We believe ours is the best game. Minor adjustments may be needed from time to time, but nobody here in the in the Office of the Commissioner is interested in making a major overhaul.

Anyway, thanks for your ideas.

Best regards,

Richard Levin
Executive Director, Public Relations

RL/dcm

P.O. Box 9368
Colo. Springs, CO 80932
October 9, 1993

Consumer Affairs
Pepperidge Farm, Inc.
Norwalk, CT 06856

Dear Cookie Captains,

Good gracious, your cookies are superb! I "discovered" them last year (November 17), and soon became fully addicted. All of your cookies are delicious, but I'm partial to the "Distinctive Geneva" variety! They are fairly orgasmic! Never before has anyone combined sweet chocolate (sugar, chocolate liquor, cocoa butter, soy lecithin, vanilla extract), unbleached enriched wheat flour (flour, niacin, reduced iron, thiamine mononitrate, riboflavin), pecans, partially hydrogenated vegetable shortening (soybean, cottonseed and/or canola oils), cornstarch, nonfat milk, invert syrup, coconut, leavening (baking soda, cream of tartar), salt, and caramel color in such a scrumptious way!! A standing ovation is certainly what you deserve and...okay, I'm going to give you one *now*......................................(fifteen seconds elapsed). There, that felt good!

But for awhile, all was not well on the Rosa home front One often hears a glowing description of something as being "better than sex." That always seemed absurd to me as my sex life has been totally satisfying for some fourteen years. My wife (Sarah Anne) and I have always devoted ourselves fully to pleasing one another and the results have been marvelous! But that all changed last year when I discovered your tremendous cookies. I often found myself sitting in front of the television for seven hours, eating two or three boxes of "Distinctive Genevas." That's 30-45 cookies, but it's virtually impossible to stop munching them, damn it! They're so good I could (and sometimes do) scream! At the beginning of this year I began to prefer eating Pepperidge Farm Cookies to having sex with my wife. At first I assumed it was just a mid-life crisis, but the scattered, empty cookie boxes told a different, tragic story, my friends Soon I had ballooned to approximately 330 pounds -I stand 5'8"- and was sleeping on the family room couch. The sex stopped completely on March 17. I had become repulsive to my wife, and foolishly increased my cookie intake to four boxes daily. In July of this year, I finally decided to take action, as I am an educated man.

Sarah Anne and I began to see a marriage counselor and our situation soon improved. Dr. Krugerson explained that I was swallowing the aggression (cookies!) that had been building up inside of me for many years. You see, my father smacked me around quite a bit when I was a child, and the healing process had never occurred. But I soon managed to confront dad -the fistfight was an unexpected but therapeutic surprise- and the marriage began to miraculously heal itself. My cookie consumption and weight are quite manageable now, and the sex with my wife is again out of this world. Yahoo and yippee!

I'm curious if you've heard similar stories. Please let me know the impact of your super cookies on other people and *their* healing processes (if it's not confidential). I don't blame your company, as the problem was with my broken heart. One mustn't blame the rose for the thorn! I await your swift reply, my friends!

Where is Pepperidge Farm?

Paul Rosa

Paul C. Rosa

PEPPERIDGE FARM, INCORPORATED • NORWALK, CONNECTICUT 06856 • TELEPHONE (203) 846-7000

November 3, 1993

Mr. Paul C. Rosa
P.O. Box 9368
Colo. Springs, CO 80932

Dear Mr. Rosa:

Thank you for contacting Pepperidge Farm. Many people are
quick to complain, but few will take the time and interest to
offer a word of praise. We therefore place a special value on
a compliment such as yours.

I am pleased to learn how much you enjoy our Geneva Cookies.
Right from its start in the 1930's, Pepperidge Farm has tried
to produce both delicious and nutritious baked goods that
would appeal to discriminating tastes. We use the finest
natural ingredients; and our baking procedures require the
utmost care. Since we put a great deal of effort into our
products, we are pleased to learn that this effort is
appreciated.

Enclosed are cents-off coupons you may use toward the
purchases of our products. Thank you again for your kind
words, and for the compliment you pay us by using our products.

                    Sincerely,

                    Ellie Eng
                    Ellie Eng
                    Manager, Consumer Affairs

508730

P.O. Box 9368
Colo. Springs, CO 80932
October 10, 1993

Mrs. Sara Werlinich, Principal
Forbes Elementary School
5785 Saltsburg Rd.
Verona, PA 15147

Dear Boss of Teachers,

Here comes a voice from the past! I attended Forbes Elementary School from 1967 to 1973. I enjoyed my time there, growing from a frightened, young child into a confident, aspiring, older child. I still have fond memories of my teachers: Mrs. Allison, Mrs. Wood, Mrs. Rose?, Mrs. Matha, Mr. Rumbaugh, and Mr. Lazar. I also liked the gym teacher, Miss Roni (she was pretty) and Principal Vollero (he wasn't). Are some *still* there? Do you know their whereabouts? My sister, Nicole, who attended Forbes (65'-71'), still thinks warmly of the school as well. While reflecting on Forbes over linguini last night, I decided to write.

I attended Seneca Junior High School, Linton Intermediate, and Penn Hills Senior High, before graduating from Penn State in 1984. Since then, I've prospered in my career as a bandanna designer and am raising eight adopted sons (Lou, Jed, Lonnie, Anwar, Rudi, Wyatt, Ed, and Pele) with my lovely wife, Bo. We also have two collies, Max and Earl, and some fish (unnamed). Life in Colorado Springs is splendid, and we have a view of majestic Pikes Peak (elev. 14,000 feet!) from our back porch. The winter months are spent snow- shoeing while summer is passed with bocci and hunting (grouse, quail). But I'm babbling!

Frankly, something has troubled me since the spring of 1969. It was a poignant time in our country's history - Vietnam protests raged while rock and roll triumphed at Woodstock- and I experienced a bit of unpleasantness. At recess one day, I was sweating heavily during a kickball game, and decided to peel off my brand new blue-jean jacket. Placing it behind home plate, I never saw it again. After the game I forgot to pick it up, and by the time I remembered to retrieve it, it was gone. My parents were livid, as the jacket cost them a pretty penny, and I had to wear a shabby cloth coat until Christmas. I was too ashamed to tell Mrs. Wood about my loss, and put the incident behind me...until this month!

"Perhaps the jacket made it to the lost-and-found box and is *still* there, waiting to be claimed!" I said to Nicole yesterday, as I ladled clam sauce onto my pasta. It had my name on the collar and probably some Bazooka Bubble Gum in the pockets. It was <u>very</u> special to me! Could you check if it's there, ma'am (I know the odds are against it)? Stranger things have happened - Robin Leach actually is popular! I look forward to your rapid reply, my friend! Oh, by the way, do you have any XL (adult) Forbes T-shirts? That would be a kick!

Elementary, Mrs. Werlinich!

Paul Rosa

Paul C. Rosa (alumnus)

SCHOOL DISTRICT OF PENN HILLS

FORBES ELEMENTARY SCHOOL
5785 Saltsburg Road
Verona, Pennsylvania 15147

Phone: 793-2155

Sara A. Werlinich
Principal

John M. Thompson
Teaching Associate Principal

IMPROVED OPPORTUNITIES FOR ALL

January 13, 1994

Dear Mr. Rosa:

Thank you for your interest in Forbes Elementary. It is always good to hear from graduates of our elementary school, especially those who have fond memories of their time here. All the teachers you mentioned have retired or changed buildings; however, one of the retired teachers visited and did recall having you as a student.

The bad news is that you will never see your blue jeans jacket again. The building policy is to turn all lost and found items over to the Penn Hills Service Association at the end of every school year. The thought that a needy child had a blue jean jacket that he/she could not otherwise afford should give you some consolation.

The Forbes staff, shared your letter, and we were fascinated with your job as a bandanna designer. There was not one among us who knew or knows of anyone else who does this for a living. We are always looking for resource people to inspire our students and hope that we can count on you.

The next time you are in the neighborhood, please stop and share your talents with us. Bring samples! In the meantime, the students and staff are practicing your vocational endeavor. Enclosed is a bandanna design sample from each of us.

We look forward to a visit and further communications.

Sincerely,

Mrs. Sara A. Werlinich
Principal

Bemis Art School
30 West Dale St.
Colorado Springs, CO 80903

Dear Fellow Artists,

My life began in the year 1971. I was raised an only child in Enfield, CT (pop. 12,900) by Curtis and Sylvia Rosa, a pair of overbearing, neurotic tyrants. I was groomed to be a guidance counselor (like my father), and graduated from high school with a 3.96 grade point average. When my parents were away from home (rarely), I would disappear into the attic and joyously practice my sketching for hours on end. Only then could I set my heart free and allow my mind to soar like a glorious peacock butterfly. But I would never share my work with my parents, as they forbade me to pursue anything artistic. They claimed creativity was the work of "Satan, the dark lord." So I would work on a project, admire it sadly for a few minutes, then quickly destroy it. Such was my lot in life.

Mom and Dad insisted I commute to a college near home, so they could continue to monitor my Christian progress. I relented and dutifully attended Wallerman University, where I (unhappily) studied Management and Human Resources as my father ordered. Living at home was quite frustrating, since my parents wouldn't permit me to go to social events or date. "All girls are evil at that age!" my mother insisted, as she served me another portion of dry meat loaf. On graduation day (June 10 of this year) I spoke to the senior class as valedictorian. In the middle of my speech -it was written by Dad- I experienced a divine intervention. The years of abuse from my parents suddenly reached a critical point, and I decided to make a break from them in front of 3,500 startled onlookers. I cleared my throat in mid-speech, adjusted the microphone, and loudly uttered the words that would change my life forever: "Mom, Dad...go **f**k** yourselves!!" I then calmly strode to the Greyhound station in my cap and gown, boarded a bus (at random), and headed for Colorado.

Well, it's now four months later, I've been properly "de-virginized" by my girlfriend, Agnes, and am happily working as a ranch hand. My parents are now a distant, pathetic memory. And I've begun sketching again, my friends! I've done over 150 drawings in recent months, and Agnes thinks I've become quite good. Now I want to show my bastard father that I was *born* to be an artist, damn it! As I understand that you give excellent art lessons, I thought I'd inquire about classes to perfect my craft. I've enclosed one of my better drawings for your (critical!) review, and hope to hear from you very soon. Also, do you have (XL) T-shirts?

Hoping to switch careers,

Paul Rosa

Paul C. Rosa

encl: One sketch submitted for review and self-addressed, stamped envelope (SASE).

RUNNING HORSE (ALBUQUERQUE)

©1993, Paul Rosa

November 29, 1993

Mr. Paul Rosa
P.O. Box 9368
Colo. Springs, CO 80932

Dear Mr. Rosa:

Please accept my apology for the delay in giving you a critique on your artwork. Time simply got away from me and I quite literally forgot about your request.

To begin with --- you should know that you have quite an amazing talent. We deal with many students here at Bemis Art School every year and it is very seldom that we run across a talent such as yours. You have retained the childlike qualities of innocence and wonderment in your work. The line quality you exhibited in your drawing shows remarkable sensitivity to the spirit of the equine nature. It is reminiscent of Picasso's later work at its very best. The textures exhibited in the mane and tail areas are wonderfully executed giving a sense of their hirsute nature. The eye and nostril areas were also done with great confidence. The only place where my staff (and myself) saw some need for growth was around the area of the hooves and the eyebrow. They exhibit hesitation and, perhaps, some latent anger. However, your choice of colors and line to suggest movement are nothing short of genius.

As for your future, I think your horizons are unlimited! In fact, I suggest that you give the Director of our Taylor Museum a call. I know that she and her Museum Committee would be interested in seeing your portfolio for possible purchase. They are always on the lookout for new talent and scenes of the American West. I know that they would consider your work a wonderful addition to our collections. Her name is Cathy Wright and I am certain that she would look forward to meeting you and seeing the rest of your work.

If that isn't to your taste, I suggest that you consider a career in writing. Your paragraphs and verbal imagery are strong. We could make use of your talents in our underwriting and grantsmanship department. There is always a need for a person of your caliber in that area. The person to contact in that department is Lori Spaulding. She would be most happy to pass on the majority of her work into your very capable hands.

I hope that these suggestions will assist you in making your career choices. Mr. Rosa --- you certainly have an exciting future to look forward to. Good luck to you.

Sincerely,

Judith Ann Polus, Director
Bemis Art School, CSFAC

Enclosure

P.S. If all else fails, you could always apply for a receptionist's position at the Fine Arts Center. There are always openings there. As an added incentive, I understand that they are now giving new recruits in that area an XL Bemis T-shirt for simply lasting out one day on the job! WHAT A DEAL!!!

P.P.S. I'm returning your artwork to you. As with all artists, I'm certain it was very difficult for you to part with it and I know you would appreciate its safe return.

Hasta la bye bye ...

P.O. Box 9368
Colo. Springs, CO 80932
October 11, 1993

Customer Concerns
Liquid-Plumr Drain Opener
The Clorox Company
Oakland, CA 94612

Dear Hairball Abolishers,

For eight years I have faithfully used your terrific product to clear my drains of dirt, sludge, filth, scum, crud, slime, muck, slop, squalor, silt, mire, offal, spawn, sediment, putridity and those annoying little pieces of soap that break off from the bar. Usually ten ounces of your magic solution is all it takes to get the water flowing as smoothly as my uncle's disability payments! You are to be held in high esteem, my accomplished friends!

Last Thursday (10/7/93) I had an experience that may be of interest to your organization. My son's pet hamster (Timi) disappeared from his cage that morning and was later found motionless in the drain of our downstairs bathtub. Tragically, the little creature had perished and we attempted to extract it with a variety of utensils. But Timi was lodged <u>very</u> tightly in the hole (probably the reason for his demise), and we were unwilling to "spear" him, if you will. A plumber would probably have charged $150 to remove the rodent, so we decided (unhappily) to give Liquid-Plumr a try. I poured about sixteen ounces of the liquid over the carcass, before quickly exiting the premises to avoid witnessing the unpleasant results. Twenty minutes later I skeptically returned to the scene of the experiment and was elated to discover that the drain was as clean as the Pope's driving record! I flushed some water through the system and was convinced that Timi was gone forever. My son (Waylon) was never told about the incident and (blissfully) believes his hamster is in "animal heaven." It certainly was an upsetting event, but it proves again that Liquid-Plumr is the best drain opener in America, and probably Europe as well. Don't let Drano steal your formula, folks!

But I'm not *entirely* pleased with your company! As an English teacher (tenth grade), I'm surprised that I didn't catch your error sooner. Amazingly, the proofreaders at your corporation never noticed that the word, "Plumber" is ***misspelled*** on the bottle (P-l-u-m-r?!). I was shocked when I spotted it for the first time recently, but assumed that it was a one-time error. But sure enough, the *next* bottle I purchased had the same mistake, and I felt it was my duty to contact you! With illiteracy at an all-time high in this country (especially in the deep south) it's inexcusable to see a mistake like this coming from a huge firm. How could this happen? Have you corrected the problem yet? Kindly let me know, so I can inform my students. Also, if you have any (XL) T-shirts, I'd be happy to own one. Please write <u>soon</u>!

P-l-u-m-b-e-r,

Paul Rosa

Paul C. Rosa

The Clorox Company

November 17, 1993

Mr. Paul C. Rosa
P.O. Box 9368
Colo. Springs, CO 80932

Dear Mr. Rosa:

Because we appreciate your taking the time to let us know how
pleased you are with our product, LIQUID-PLUMR drain opener, I am
enclosing a complimentary coupon.

Knowing that you like our product is important, and we value the
generous comments you have shared with us. As for the spelling of
product's name, it is intentionally spelled without an "e."
Because the marketing specialists working on the development of
this product are also interested in your opinion, I am forwarding
your comments to them.

Again, thank you for letting us know that our efforts have been
successful.

Sincerely,

ANGELA ALIOTO
Product Specialist

11/12/93 1067/1A 5770
AA/aa

enc: 32-ounce LIQUID-PLUMR coupon

P.O. Box 9368
Colo. Springs, CO 80932
October 12, 1993

Hall of the Presidents Wax Museum
1050 S. 21st St.
Colo. Springs, CO 80904

Dear Exhibitors,

I have something amazing I hope to submit to your fine organization, but would like to begin by explaining the reasons for my interesting endeavor. As a young boy growing up in Dyer, IN (pop. 10,500) in the 1930's and 40's, my family frequently went to various wax museums around the state. We would marvel at the glorious reproductions of Abraham Lincoln, Genghis Khan, and (my sister's favorite) Florence Nightingale! In those days the "Hoosier State" had quite a few of these attractions and we would visit them ten to twenty times each year! These visits brought our family closer together as we learned about the wonders of history.

Well, in 1941 (I was 12) I began wondering why there weren't any *ear wax museums*! My family (Mom, Dad, Tess, Agnes, and Rufus) all agreed that it was a terrific idea, and thought I should "create" the first ear wax statue. I was just a pip-squeak at the time, but I industriously got to work! Every few days I would carefully swab the insides of my ears and store the precious yield in a small tin (cigar) canister. I diligently "worked" through World War II (Rufus returned safely!), and realized this would be an *enormous* undertaking! In 1947, when I was a freshman at Yale, I finally had enough ear wax to complete a pair of feet. Only now did I decide who the subject of my masterpiece would be: **Galileo**! I was studying math and science, so it seemed fitting.

After graduation, I moved to Dallas (with Galileo's feet *and ankles*) and began my career as a physicist. And the ear wax collecting continued! By 1960 (I was now 31), Galileo's legs had been expertly sculpted, and I began to really believe that my project was possible! By 1975 (age 46), I had married my beloved Jenny and had fathered four magnificent children, and the statue grew more majestic each year! My family consistently offered to contribute *their* ear wax, but I politely declined, explaining it would diminish my accomplishment. On New Year's Eve that year, I proudly completed Galileo's torso, and soon started forming his arms.

My family and career prospered as we moved from Dallas to Chicago to Colorado Springs. The work on Galileo never stopped, and by 1982 (age 53) I was done with his arms and hands! Only the head and face still needed completing, and I began scooping my ears with a renewed fervor! Well, I'm 64 and retired, and the spectacular face of Galileo was finished one week ago! I cried when I put the final touches on his ears (an appropriate place to stop, wasn't it?). A xeroxed copy of a photograph of my creation is enclosed.

But now I'm thrilled about the possibility of sharing my achievement with the world! Are you interested in getting involved? Please write me *soon* (SASE enclosed) and let me know what you think. I'm very excited! Also, could you please send a (XL) T-shirt? God bless you!

Pass the Q-Tips,

Paul Rosa

Paul C. Rosa

HALL OF THE PRESIDENTS
LIVING WAX STUDIO

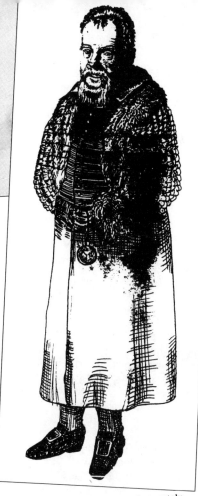

January 24, 1994

Paul C. Rosa
P.O. Box 9368
Colo. Springs, CO 80932

Dear Sir:

Thank you for sharing your lifetime endeavor with us. It sounds like an interesting project, unfortunately we have no place for it in our museum.

However, you may wish to contact

Rippley's Believe It or Not Museums
8201 International Drive
Orlando, FL 32819
Attn: Sandi Jones, PR/MKTG Dir.

Sincerely,

Grant Carey
General Manager

GLC/cjb

P.O. Box 9368
Colo. Springs, CO 80932
December 2, 1993

Ms. Diane Vlash, Consumer Information
Q-Tips Cotton Swabs
Chesebrough Pond's USA Co.
55 Merritt Boulevard
Trumbull, CT 06611

Dear Ms. Vlash,

First of all, how do you pronounce your name? Does it rhyme with posh or with M*A*S*H? Or with neither? M*A*S*H is my all time favorite television program, but that really has nothing to do with Chesebrough Pond's, does it? Nevertheless, Hawkeye, Klinger, Hot Lips, etc. were truly a memorable collection of characters. And now it's time to get to the point, isn't it?

For most of the past fifty years I didn't use cotton swabs because I was "saving" my earwax for a unique endeavor. Having seen plenty of wax statues as a youth, I was diligently building the first *ear wax* statue! Cotton swabs aren't good for saving ear wax, so a small wooden scoop was my instrument of choice for half a decade. As the enclosed xeroxed copy of a photograph of my creation (Galileo!) shows, my efforts were rewarded. I am currently negotiating with several corporations and hope to have my masterpiece exhibited nationwide. I feel that Q-Tips would be a perfect sponsor for the "event," and would like to hear your comments on the matter!

Finally, I would like to recommend a design change for Q-Tips! I always find that, to clean two ears effectively, requires three "swabs." That's 1.5 Q-Tip for each cleaning session, so I waste half a Q-Tip every morning (saving the "half-used" Q-Tip seems barbaric!). I asked some of my friends and most agree that it typically takes them three swabs as well. With this in mind, I would like to suggest that you change the Q-Tip design from "I" shaped" to "Y" shaped! With a "Y," one can take advantage of the three "sides" by adding an extra swab and making the typical ear clean-up a one-Q-Tip job. I have sketched a crude drawing of my idea below.

Please send me your thoughts on my innovative concept (I'm willing to sell the patent) and the ear wax statue promotion possibilities. I look forward to another swift reply!

Waxing excited,

Paul Rosa

Paul C. Rosa

Schematic:

Chesebrough-Pond's USA Co.

CONSUMER INFORMATION CENTER

55 MERRITT BOULEVARD
TRUMBULL, CT 06611

December 6, 1993

Mr. Paul Rosa
P.O. Box 9368
Colo. Springs, CO 80932

Dear Mr. Rosa:

We have received your letter and appreciate your sending us your proposal for a new product or concept as well as advising us of your "creation".

While we are always interested in new ways to meet our consumers' needs and expectations, it is our policy not to accept unsolicited ideas from outside the company.   Due to the above, we are also unable to sponsor your "ear wax statue".   We feel that it is in our best interest to have such a policy, in spite of the chance of not looking at what could be a really good idea.

The reason for this decision is that we have carefully crafted new product programs that involve a large effort in both marketing and research and development and wish to avoid misunderstandings about who might have thought of a fairly common idea or concept first.

We do, however, review patented products, after the U.S. patent has been issued, as it affords the inventor a strong measure of protection.   If and when you have a U.S. patent, please feel free to contact us.

We regret not being able to accept your idea and thank you very much for thinking of Chesebrough-Pond's.   We wish you every success in your endeavors.

Sincerely,

Walter Dabek
Walter Dabek
Director, Consumer Information

P.O. Box 9368
Colo. Springs, CO 80932
October 15, 1993

Customer Service
Avis Rental Car Company (World Headquarters)
900 Old Country Rd.
Garden City, NY 11530-9795

Dear Car Loaners,

The road is my friend. Few things in life give me more pleasure (my wife, Riki, is an exception!) than hopping into a sparkling Avis rental car (mid-size) and rollin' down that highway, putting my concerns a hundred (or more) kilometers behind me! Growing up in tidy Hancock, MS (pop. 24,537), I was always taught the meaning of "value" and "honor," and your organization clearly learned some of the same lessons! Were some of *you* raised in Hancock as well (the odds are against it)? So, keep up the outstanding work and continue to put the customer on a pedestal; we certainly enjoy the view from up there, so to speak!!

Knowing that the consumer comes first with Avis, I feel completely comfortable posing a few questions. First of all, what happens (hypothetically) if I get a parking ticket while using a rental car? Do the police really have a ghost of a chance of prosecuting the deserving party (hypothetically, me)? I doubt it, my friends. Avis doesn't help punish its customers, do they? That would be objectionable.

Also, I've heard your motto, "We try harder," for a long, long time now. If this is truly the case, why then is Hertz *still* number one?! How could you possibly "try harder" for twenty consecutive years, but never take over the number one spot? This implies that Avis simply doesn't operate as "intelligently" as Hertz, don't you agree? Otherwise, why isn't this unparalleled effort rewarded with a top ranking? I just don't get it, my friends! As this motto seems a bit silly to me, I would like to offer these possible replacements:

* Do a number two with Avis!
* It "Hertz" Avis to see you wasting money!
* Avis, safer than AMTRAK!
* To hell with parking tickets! Go Avis!
* It's time for _**Avis**it_ to your mother's house!

So, please get back to me on the above issues as soon as you can (knowing Avis, I expect a letter very soon). The mottos are yours at no charge! By the way, are you hiring advertising executives right now? Lastly, do you have any (XL) T-shirts? That would be cool! Adios!

Bursting with ideas,

Paul Rosa

Paul C. Rosa

AVIS

An Employee-Owned Company

**Avis Rent A Car
System, Inc.**

World Headquarters
900 Old Country Road
Garden City, New York 11530

Telephone: (516) 222-3000
Fax: (516) 222-4381

January 20, 1994

Mr. Paul C Rosa
P.O. Box 9368
Colo. Springs, CO 80932

Dear Mr. Rosa:

Sorry that we are so late in responding to your thoughtful
letter. The first one either went astray or did not get here
at all.

Thank you for the many compliments, and I'll try answering
the questions that you posed:

1. As to parking tickets, just as with their personal
cars, renters are responsible for any traffic infractions.

2. Our "We try harder." slogan has made Avis a
household word around the world, and we wouldn't dream of
dropping it. We try harder to be the best, not necessarily
the biggest car rental company; best in quality service
delivery to our customers, best in financial health, and best
with a dedicated employee-owner workforce.

3. We have a very small advertising staff here, which
oversees our outside agencies, but if we decide to expand,
we'll be in touch.

4. Accompanying this letter are two XL T-shirts to
thank you for writing us.

Sincerely,

*2 X-L
T-shirts
Received!!*

Raymond C. Noble
Public Relations Manager

RCN/jal

P.S. We don't know of anyone up here that hails from your
hometown, but surely there is someone nearby at our
Mississippi rental location who is.

P.O. Box 9368
Colo. Springs, CO 80932
October 16, 1993

Consumer Affairs
Liquid Paper Correction Fluid
The Gillette Company
Stationery Products Division, Box 61
Boston, MA 02199

Dear Error Obscurers,

Liquid Paper is a godsend! Although I generally use a computer for my letter-writing needs, I still do quite a bit of corresponding in the written format (it's more personal). Obviously this approach (writing) has its drawbacks since one can't personally "erase" an error as neatly as the computer can. That's when Liquid Paper steps in and saves the day, my friends! I thoroughly enjoy the process of dipping the delicate, little brush into the fluid and "painting" the mistake into oblivion! As an award-winning abstract artist, the creative use of paint is important to me. And I always marvel at the wonderful technology available today!

But I am prone to chronic bouts of clumsiness, and for this reason (indirectly) I felt compelled to contact you. Some of my writing errors are so disastrous that the small paint brushes provided with the Liquid Paper prove woefully inadequate. I propose that you also offer some bottles with paint ***rollers*** and other bottles with a convenient ***spray paint*** option (for huge mistakes). Obscuring mangled text with a quick "roll" or press of a button would be magnificent! What do you think?

Furthermore, I have begun working with Liquid Paper in my art studio, and find the consistency of your paint to be absolutely superior! Frankly, it is the finest paint I've used to date! Therefore, I was wondering if I could purchase your product in larger quantities (quart or gallon containers) for my creative endeavors. As it is, the tiny bottles are simply too expensive and inconvenient. A gallon of Liquid Paper costs about $350 (213.33 bottles!). That's enough to bankrupt a fellow and drive him crazy too, as he attempts to manage the countless, minuscule containers.

Lastly, as I am truly indebted to you folks, I decided to submit one of my recent artistic creations, suitable for framing and hanging on a wall at your corporate headquarters. Entitled "Moonscape," it was completed in a particularly focused six-day period last month. I would welcome your comments on my creation and the above topics as well. I anxiously await your reply. And (I almost forgot) do you have (XL) T-shirts? Farewell!

Louvre,

Paul Rosa

Paul C. Rosa

"MOONSCAPE" —P. Rosa 93

The Gillette Company
P.O. Box 61
Boston, Massachusetts 02199

November 8, 1993

Mr. Paul Rosa
P.O. Box 9368
Colo. Springs, CO 80932

Dear Mr. Rosa:

Thank you for your very thoughtful and kind comments. It's wonderful to know how much you like Liquid Paper Correction Fluid.

Your compliments and suggestions are being shared with all the people who work on Liquid Paper. You can be sure everyone will be pleased to know that their efforts are appreciated.

I am enclosing a coupon for Liquid Paper - Bond White as a small token of our thanks for taking the time to share your feelings with us. Please call me on our toll-free number, 1-800-Gillette (445-5388) if you ever have any questions or other comments you want to share about Gillette products.

Sincerely,

Mark Rideout
Consumer Service Representative

P.O. Box 9368
Colo. Springs, CO 80932
October 17, 1993

The Evan Marshall Literary Agency
22 South Park St., Suite 216
Montclair, NJ 07042-2744

Dear Book Bunch,

I just got done writing me a real funny book, and thought I would let you know about it! If you like the idea I'm about to tell you about, maybe we can hook up and make us some good money together. That would be real great, wouldn't it? I'm thinking that we can make a total of $500,000 dollars, and I'd let you have about half of that. I think that's pretty fair.

Anyways, my 47 page story is about geese and ducks and how damn funny they can be if you take some time to get to know em' all! Last year I noticed that they can do some histerical stuff and no body wrote a story about em yet, so I thought I should give it a shot. Since I was knee high to my daddys cows down in Cottonport, LA (pop. 1911) I figured I could write me something funny. My high school teacher Mr. Stein (I figure he was a Jewish fella) told me I was pretty good with my words and should try to do some writing in my spair time. When I started thinking about them geese and ducks I knew I had me an idea that was a good one. So I bought me a used computer with my extra towtrucking money and got to typing!

I think people will really laugh hard at my book about the funny ways ducks and geese walk and act when they are swiming around and stuff in a pond or lake. When you feed a bunch of them, they all fight and squawk and make a ruckus cause they wanna be the only one to get some food. They look funny as hell when they walk on the sidewalk and I mentioned that funny phrase that says "he looks like a duck out of water"! That is such a true thing don't you think so? I also wrote about how ducks and geese look so funny when they fly around and try to fly south. It's funny as heck that they fly in the shape of a big V cause they think that it will cut down on wind resistance or something. They are so stupid! and funny too! Sometimes them birds will get mad at a person and try to peck or bite him and that's the funniest cause they only weigh about ten pounds and a lot of folks weigh more than 200! That's not a fair fight and it's so funny it almost makes me cry sometimes!! My great book also talks about how they don't even stop when they go to the bathroom! They just keep on walking like nothings happening at all! Man, that cracks me up so much!

I don't have much experience writing books, but I like to write a lot of letters and I think I'm as funny as that Woody Alen fella or that Dave Barry too. I don't know about Gallager the comedian though. When he smashes watermelons with his big hammer I'm on the floor rolling and laughing. So get back to me and let me know what you think! I'm putting in a envelope that already has a stamp so you don't have to worry about it. I'm so exited about selling my book which is called "Those funny birds!" and I'll talk to you soon!

Thank you kindly for reading my letter to you,

Paul Rosa

Paul C. Rosa

P.S. Do you have XL T shirts? I like to colect them things!

The Evan Marshall Agency

22 SOUTH PARK STREET, SUITE 216
MONTCLAIR, NJ 07042-2744
TEL (201) 744-1661   FAX (201) 744-6312

Evan Marshall
President

October 25, 1993

Mr. Paul Rosa
P.O. Box 9368
Colo. Springs, CO 80932

Dear Mr. Rosa:

Thank you for your letter of October 17. Unfortunately, your
book does not sound right for us, but I wish you success with
it.

Sincerely,

EM:nmb

P.O. Box 9368
Colo. Springs, CO 80932
October 18, 1993

Mr. Bruce Tracy, Editor
Doubleday & Co., Inc.
1540 Broadway
New York, NY 10036

Dear Mr. Tracy (Do you have a brother named "Dick?"),

First of all, I would like to apologize for the bad joke. No doubt you've heard it over 4,200 times and are rather sick of it. If I had any decency whatsoever I'd backtrack and use the handy "delete" function on my keyboard to eliminate what's in parentheses above. However, if I did *this*, the preceding three sentences would make no sense whatsoever, so I have chosen (after much introspection) to instead continue with this epistle.

As you know, Doubleday has purchased the right to publish my book of letters to corporations nationwide (with the responses) and I am delighted indeed. When my agent (Lisa) told me the good news I proceeded to play my favorite Cat Stevens 8-Track Tape ("Teaser and the Firecat") and dance madly about my cramped apartment in a pair of flannel pajamas. Although I frightened my cat (Jesse) almost to death, it was well worth the effort. I hadn't been that excited since my momentous high school prom (note: the theme was "Romance amongst the ivy"). When I told my parents (Lou and Selenasovitch) the good news they exclaimed, "Don't forget, you owe us money!" Unconditional family support is pivotal in a young man's emotional development, wouldn't you say, Mr. Tracy (is "Bruce" too...forward?)?

Since this is the first volume I have sold, I thought it would be prudent to pose a few consequential questions regarding its presentation (and such). As I assume you are a busy man, I will immediately proceed to the very queries alluded to a mere one sentence ago:

1. Wouldn't it be inventive to print the book on tiny pages (3" x 2.5")? I firmly believe that a convenient "pocket-size" version will sell extraordinarily well!
2. May I mention (in the Preface) that the entire book was actually conceived by my aforementioned cat, and that I merely acted as a "medium?"
3. How about including a slice of American cheese with each book? Mercy, e<u>veryone</u> enjoys cheese, Bruce!
4. May I stay in your guest room when I visit New York?

I would be grateful if you took a few moments and "tapped out" some thoughts on your trusty word processor. I have thoughtfully enclosed a handy, self-addressed, stamped envelope (HSASE). Frankly, I don't understand why "self-addressed" is always mentioned. Whom else would it be addressed to? Perhaps that can serve as question number five, my friend!

Meticulously,

Paul Rosa

Paul C. Rosa, Scribe

Doubleday
Bantam Doubleday Dell

November 1, 1993

Mr. Paul Rosa
P. O. Box 9368
Colorado Springs CO 80932

Dear Mr. Rosa,

Thank you for your letter of October 18. I, too, am pleased that Doubleday will publish your book of letters. It is always a happy occurrence when author, editor, agent, and publisher share enthusiasm, vision, spirit, and a contract with option.

Your suggestion of printing the book on very small pages is an intriguing one. A small volume might suggest a chapbook, prayer book, or diary. This format would very much support your book's leitmotif as a sort of *vade mecum* for the consumer, a marketplace manifesto for the capitalist citizen. However, I fear the small size might render the letters difficult to read, thus diminishing their intertextual resonance, the neo-gospel call-and-response of epistolary exchange.

You may indeed mention your cat in the book. Dedication, acknowledgment, and homage to the muse are all estimable literary conventions, older than movable type. I would, however, recommend that your mention of Jesse not be species-specific.

The idea of including a slice of cheese with each copy of the book is a bold and masterful stroke on your part--a semiotic *double entendre*, a metaphoric *coup de grace*--*i.e.*, to include in a meditation on the consumer/vendor dynamic an American *ur*product, pasteurized, processed, and individually wrapped. Unfortunately, however, the inclusion of perishable items in published books is still an unrealizable dream, as they tend to decompose and foul our warehouse.

I look forward to receiving the complete manuscript as much, I'm sure, as you look forward to receiving the money due you when it is delivered.

Sincerely,

Bruce Tracy
Senior Editor

P.O. Box 9368
Colo. Springs, CO 80932
October 29, 1993

Nicole Rosa, "Sister"
160 Glenfield Dr.
Colo. Springs, CO 80968

Dear Nicole ("Nicki"),

Hello. Although you live a mere three miles from me, I thought it would prove beguiling to correspond by mail. Granted, a letter that travels only three miles could make an already disgruntled postal employee snap like an autumn twig and open fire on innocent citizens from atop the city's tallest structure (Holly Sugar Building) with a cache of deadly, illegal automatic weapons. But if I know you (and I do), your response is, "The chances of the postal employee hitting *me* are remote!" I'll proceed.

You're adopted. Mom and Dad told me to **never** mention this to anyone, especially you, but it's time you learned the truth. Apparently you were abandoned as a seven-month-old baby at the edge of a park in Canton, OH (pop. 94,730) during the summer of 1960. A pack of wild poodles happened upon your prone, gurgling form, whisking you away, into the woods, where you were reared as "one of the pack." You soon grew fat and content on poodle milk, road kill, and partially eaten Whoppers (pilfered from Burger King dumpsters). Nicki, you learned the "language" of the poodle, the hierarchy of the pack (*never* anger the Alpha Poodle), and the importance of group hunting skills. Surprisingly, the other dogs didn't object to your presence, lovingly embracing you as one of their own. Perhaps they even looked up to you because seven years to them was only one to you ("Our fellow pack member has the power to slow down time!" they might have thought). But your blissful days of canine camaraderie ended abruptly in the late winter of 1963. Brace yourself, "sister," as I conclude this riveting tale!

On the night of February 16, 1963 the pack, emaciated from a long, brutal winter, ventured from "the lair" and headed for downtown Canton to secure a meal of some sort. Typically, Nicki, you clung to the back of your mother ("Kimba") as she dashed across the frozen tundra. At the edge of the woods Kimba, misjudging the space beneath a tree branch, "allowed" your skull to connect with the offending extremity. As your soft, pliant forehead met the rigid limb (at approximately forty miles per hour) you were torn free from Kimba's pelt, falling to the earth with a sickening thud. The dogs surrounded you as you writhed in confusion and agony. As *any* poodle pack is concerned with the purity of the breed, they quickly abandoned you as a "reject." Shortly thereafter, a Mr. and Mrs. John Rosa, hiking through the woods, happened upon your dazed person. Soon you were officially adopted, and the barks, yelps and yowls were transformed into passable words. This is your dramatic history, Nicki.

I am willing to tell you more, but perhaps that's enough for now. I encourage a response in the enclosed SASE ("Sassy") and request a (XL) T-shirt. Finally, please stop burying bones in my garden!

I'll *never* call you "bitch,"

Paul Rosa

Paul C. Rosa

160 Glenfield Dr.
Colo. Springs, CO 80968
November 14, 1993

Paul Rosa
P.O. Box 9368
Colo. Springs, CO 80932

Dear Paul,

Sigh. Your story was, at best, mildly amusing, and could only be described as yet another pathetic display of sibling rivalry. Why you have not yet outgrown this tendency, at your advanced age, is quite a mystery to me. I must applaud you, as this is the wildest stretch of reality you've concocted to date. Last week you were determined to convince me that Dad liked you better than me, because he shipped you your tennis trophies and chucked my horse show ribbons in the dumpster. Did you really think I could not verify this scenario with a quick phone call back home? Not only did our father assure me that this was utter hogwash, but he confided in me that you did not actually win those tennis trophies at all. He actually bribed your opponents, most of them elder, respected members of the greater Pittsburgh business community, to let you win, in order to give your underdeveloped and lagging self-esteem a much needed boost. The trouble dear Papa went to, to set this charade up, not to mention keeping it hidden from you, was really quite touching, and entirely beyond the scope of normal fatherhood. So fragile was your ego and self-esteem. But enough, I do not wish to upset you any further.

The fact of the matter is that I was born first. It was bliss until you came along, what with your whining, blubbering and diaper degradation. You were such a sensitive, needy child, that I could barely stand the sight of you, wallowing uselessly in your crib, and it took quite a bit of self-control on my part, to keep from snapping your silly little neck. But of course I never harmed a hair on your shiny little head, and became the picture of perfect sister-dom. It was you who could never stand the thought of my two years of undivided attention from Mom and Dad, before you were born. You dwelled upon this notion, letting it fester inside you, making you quite an intolerable and wretched little boy. Mom and Dad humored you, consoling themselves with the thought that you'd eventually outgrow these jealous tendencies, and come to love and respect your older sister for the fine human being she is. But, alas, this was not to happen. Almost weekly I am plagued with vicious phone calls, late-night telegrams, and hurtful letters such as this latest debacle. I see that 19 years of analysis was completely wasted on you. Brother dear, I shall always love you, since we come from the same loins, but I must ask you (once again) to steer clear of my life!

I don't even like dogs,

Nicole E. Rosa
Nicole E. Rosa

P.S. Get your own (XL) t-shirt. I'm tired of you always wearing my hand-me-downs.

P.O. Box 9368
Colo. Springs, CO 80932
January 21, 1994

Personal Feelings Department
Paul Rosa
P.O. Box 9368
Colo. Springs, CO 80932

Dear Mr. Rosa (Oh, what the hell..."Paul!")

As you well know, you have spent a great deal of time -perhaps too much time- writing letters recently to corporations nationwide. During the last several months you have contacted Pizza Hut, Ivory Soap, Safeway, Arm & Hammer, Caterpillar, Xerox (Xerox), Hallmark, Oprah and many others. When you didn't receive a reply within six weeks you aggressively re-submitted the letter or sent a follow-up message. Good gracious, Paul, you spent a small fortune on envelopes and postage!

Don't you have anything better to do than whiling the (valuable) hours away in front of your computer, with The Late Show often blaring in the background? Is there some passionate, underlying reason for the many hours devoted to this odd venture? Perhaps you were laid off by a large, impersonal company once and this is your "revenge." Maybe you are incredibly lonely and this is your way of maintaining limited contact with the outside world. Are you fascinated with stamps? Or do you simply enjoy annoying hard-working, well-meaning, well-groomed customer service employees? Many would consider this to be unusual behavior, my friend, and I hoped to hear *your* feelings on this intriguing topic.

Finally, as a "fact nut," I would like to gather some poignant data:

1. How did you achieve such a high rate of response on your letters?
2. In general, how do you feel about the replies?
3. Do you like eggs?
4. How many T-shirts did you receive?
5. What *else* do you do with your time?
6. What do you hope to do in the future?

Please respond to my above questions, Paul, as I am a man who devours facts and knowledge as though they were White Castle hamburgers. I have heedfully enclosed a self-addressed, stamped envelope (self-addressed, stamped envelope) for your convenience. And, as a final gesture of good will, please send a (XL) T-shirt. You are a decent fellow!

Conclusively,

Paul Rosa

Paul C. Rosa

P.O. Box 9368
Colo. Springs, CO 80932
January 26, 1994

Mr. Paul Rosa
P.O. Box 9368
Colo. Springs, CO 80932

Dear Mr. Rosa,

Thank you for your charming letter of January 21, 1994. Many folks have inquired about the nature of my letters, but your queries were the most insightful yet! I'll get straight to the point.

In June of 1993 I received a form letter from Pizza Hut's Vice President of Marketing, stating that it had been a while since I ordered a pizza from them. The letter continued by saying, "This concerns me because you're the kind of customer we'd like to see more often." I thought this was inane, as I assumed a restaurant would like to see *any* kind of customer, as long as they have money! So I decided to write and ask him, "Which kind of customer *wouldn't* you like to see more often?" Then I realized that corporations as a rule (especially through television commercials) treat the American public like idiots, saying all manner of things that sound "nice," but really mean nothing at all. An idea was born! If I was going to be *treated* like an idiot, I thought it would be fun to write letters from the *perspective* of an idiot.

Frankly, Mr. Rosa, I *don't* have anything better to do than write these letters (with David Letterman entertaining in the background). I've never had so much fun in my life! Furthermore, I believe that my "project" serves a valuable purpose. Based on the typical responses to my letters, I must point out that most corporations seem to have about as much creativity and humor as your average yam. Form letter after form letter poured in, and I was amazed at the consistency of their...dullness. I have no idea why they need to be like this, but I think it's a sad situation and should be remedied. And now, Mr. Rosa, let's address your spirited questions:

1. Many responses resulted from the merciless resubmission of letters and/or *additional* (progressively more aggressive) messages. They typically "surrender" eventually!
2. See above paragraph.
3. Yes, I love them.
4. Nine (from Imodium-AD, Xerox, US West (2), Citgo (3), and Avis (2))!
5. I'm a stand-up comic, screenwriter, and creator of the popular bumper stickers, "My Kid Beat Up Your Honor Student," "DARE To Keep Cops Off Donuts," "WHATEVER," and "I Think You Left The Stove On," all available at Spencer Gifts stores nationwide.
6. I hope to eventually be involved in the film industry. I would also like to continue authoring books, come up with more bumper stickers, and add to my extensive (XL) T-shirt collection.

I hope this answers your questions and I wish you continued success.

Stay tuned for a sequel!

Paul Rosa

Mr. Paul C. Rosa (Personal Feelings Dept.)

Paul Rosa
P.O. Box 9368
Colo. Springs, CO 80932

Mr., Mrs., or Ms. John Q. Reader (YOU!)
An Address on a Street
A City, a State, and then (obviously), a five-digit number

Dear Reader and the like,

Hello. Now that you've read approximately 160 pages of mind-numbing drivel, gibberish, jabber, foolishness, chatter, nonsense, twaddle, babble, and patter -which I hope you managed to enjoy- we (you) have arrived at the very last letter in this silly publication! To show my gratitude for your purchase, I've decided to write a letter to you "personally!" If, however, you are merely *borrowing* this book from a friend (you tightwad), I suggest you dash to your local bookstore immediately and <u>buy</u> a copy of your very own! You see, conclusive studies at a fairly large university indicated that this book will triple in value in the year 1998, and again in 2006, just like Hal Linden's autograph! But if you don't *want* a copy, I urge you to instead invest in a quality garment. See ya' in the next paragraph...

After receiving many (nine) T-shirts from generous corporations from coast to coast (if you will), I decided it would be splendid to offer you (the reader) a T-shirt as well! After carefully deliberating for several seconds whether I should give them away for free, I bellowed, "Hell, no, that would be <u>extremely</u> stupid, Paul! I bet some people would actually send money!" This shouted, I proceeded to take a soothing, hot shower. Then, freshly scrubbed, I concluded it would be cool (as the kids say) to produce a quality T-shirt featuring a nifty design similar to the cover of this book. Prudently contacting a clothing manufacturer, I arranged to have said garments printed on the east coast (part of it...the coast, that is). I'm dropping down to paragraph "C."

Still here? Anyway, if this magnificent garb interests you, please send $15.00 (or more) to:

Idiot Letters T-shirt Offer
c/o Baggs Humor Us Studio
P.O. Box 487
Ocean City, MD 21842

Checks should be made payable to "Baggs Humor Us Studio," and all proceeds will go to the preservation of...um, some very old trees and things in Connecticut and an important museum in southern Idaho devoted to the further understanding of tiny mollusks. For God's sake, won't you please help?! Whether you would like a shirt or not, I appreciate that you read my first book! Now I ask that you wrap your arms around yourself (pretending it's me) in a loving hug and mumble (again, imagining it's me): "Thanks plenty for your attention and I hope you enjoyed it!" Adios, friends!

Fighting Tears,

Paul Rosa

Paul C. (Charles) Rosa